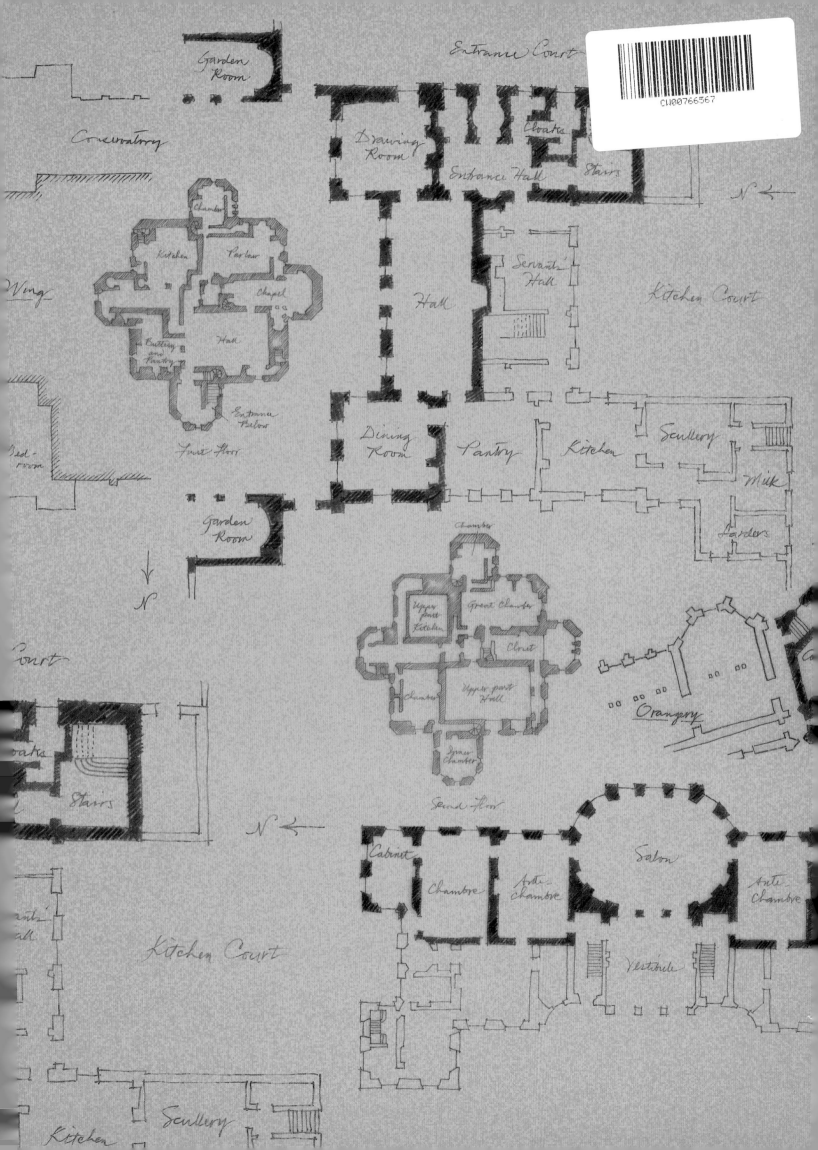

— THE LIFE OF THE HOUSE —

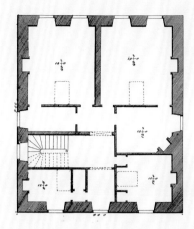

Henrietta Spencer-Churchill

THE LIFE OF

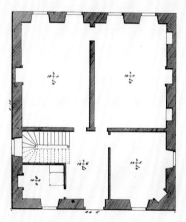

THE HOUSE

How Rooms Evolve

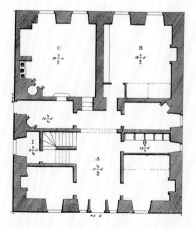

RIZZOLI
NEW YORK

New York · Paris · London · Milan

First published in the
United States of America in 2012
by Rizzoli International Publications, Inc.
300 Park Avenue South, New York, NY 10010

www.rizzoliusa.com

2012 2013 2014 2015 2016 / 10 9 8 7 6 5 4 3 2 1

Edited by Alexandra Parsons
Designed and typeset in Fleischman by Dalrymple
Printed and bound in China
Distributed to the US trade by Random House

ISBN: 978-0-8478-3856-1

Library of Congress Control Number 2012938045

Endpapers drawn by Conrad Villamar

EVEN as a young child I had immense curiosity about houses. Not only the history of who had lived in them, but how, when and why the houses themselves had changed. I was often found wandering off to explore. I'd find hidden staircases and creep into the attics or deep basement caverns, and when playing hide and seek I was never found, as I always knew the best places to hide! That fascination with the evolution of houses and the rooms and spaces within them has continued, based on my interest in architecture as well as in social history that forces change.

In this book I try to give an overview of the main architectural features and layouts of rooms from medieval times to present day, and to pinpoint some of the social and industrial advances which led to these changes. I look at alterations room by room, showing how lifestyles and trends have contributed to the way in which we use certain rooms today. A good example is the move from kitchens run purely by servants in the basement to large live-in family kitchens occupying a prime position in the house. I also explore how, with the introduction of internal plumbing, bathrooms could be installed whilst maintaining the integrity of the building and architectural features, often a problem we still face today.

As this is such a vast subject, I have concentrated largely on English houses and examples of American equivalents where appropriate and important. I have included both houses that I have worked on as a designer, and thus experienced firsthand the real problems and challenges, and also some houses that have important historical family relevance for me such as Blenheim, my family home in England, and Marble House in Newport, Rhode Island, where my great-grandmother Consuelo Vanderbilt spent much of her childhood.

My hope is that through this book you will see how it is possible for houses and rooms to evolve in a practical way through the centuries, yet retain the character of the particular era in which they were built, revealing even more of the lives and lifestyles of those who lived in them.

Henrietta Spencer-Churchill

ARCHITECTURE

ERIODS are defined by their architecture, and the interiors of homes – grand, modest and humble – are in their turn influenced by the dictates of the times in which they were built: by available technologies, by life's necessities and by fashion. So it is that when glass is a new product, it is expensive to produce, so only the grandest homes have windows and the grandest of the grandest have the biggest and the most. When the only heat source is the wood-burning fireplace, the grandest homes have the most chimneys, and the simple cottage makes do with one hearth that serves for both cooking and heating. These restrictions dictate the nature of the spaces within. Lifestyles, too, have an influence. The collective nature of life in past times afforded few private spaces, and generations unused to privacy take their time to demand it. There is a collective taste at work, too, thanks to travel and expanding horizons, so the pendulum swings between overwrought Gothic to restrained elegance, back to decorative clutter, and away to the calm again, back to exuberance, off to simplicity and back again to the comfort zone. And all this is reflected in the busy, bustling, changing life of the rooms behind the façades.

"…We shape our buildings: thereafter they shape us."
Winston Churchill (1874–1965)
British politician and statesman

below and previous page *This house is an interesting combination of medieval, Tudor and Palladian with this façade showing the Tudor wing and part of the main Palladian façade. Internally, it was important to provide a harmonious link between the different styles whilst retaining their individual characteristics.*

Melford Hall, Norfolk, was built in the 16th Century and incorporated some of the original medieval monastery used by the abbots of Bury St. Edmunds. The layout is typical of an Elizabethan building and the red brick is typical of local building materials.

— TUDOR CONFIDENCE —

The earliest part of this house dates from 1719, and this wing was added in 1881. The windows on the ground-floor level were originally smaller and not in proportion or in the same style as the other windows, so in a recent remodelling they were changed. This has resulted in a more harmonious façade and lighter rooms inside.

THE sixteenth century saw complete contrasts in terms of style, from irregular unsymmetrical façades and skylines with a variety of Gothic and Renaissance ornament – described at the time as "a heap of craziness of decorations . . . very disgusting to see" – to balanced symmetrical classical buildings. Earlier houses were often inward-looking courtyard houses in brick with Italian Renaissance influences filtering through England via France and Flanders, characterized by decorative features such as strapwork ceilings and decorative plasterwork depicting nymphs and scrollwork.

With Britain's new Elizabethan age of prosperity, a large number of larger and smaller houses were being built with an emphasis on symmetrical outward-looking façades. Internally there was a move towards greater privacy with a series of smaller rooms leading off a now more intimate entrance hall, and rooms were built each with a specific purpose.

The open-plan great halls of the medieval period now had ceilings installed, thus creating a room above, and walls and ceilings were decorated with carved beams and decorative plasterwork and friezes. Early plasterwork consisted of simple, applied geometric features, but as the period progressed the detail and sophistication of strapwork plaster ceilings blossomed under the influence of the great Italian plasterers. Glass was now more readily available in England, so regular glass panes with stone mullions and transoms replaced Gothic stone tracery.

The fireplace was very much the focal point of the room and whilst the trend for arched windows declined, it was still a typical shape used for the head of the stone fireplace, whilst grander double-height Elizabethan rooms were dominated by giant carved fireplaces with elaborate over-mantels with heraldic carvings and columns.

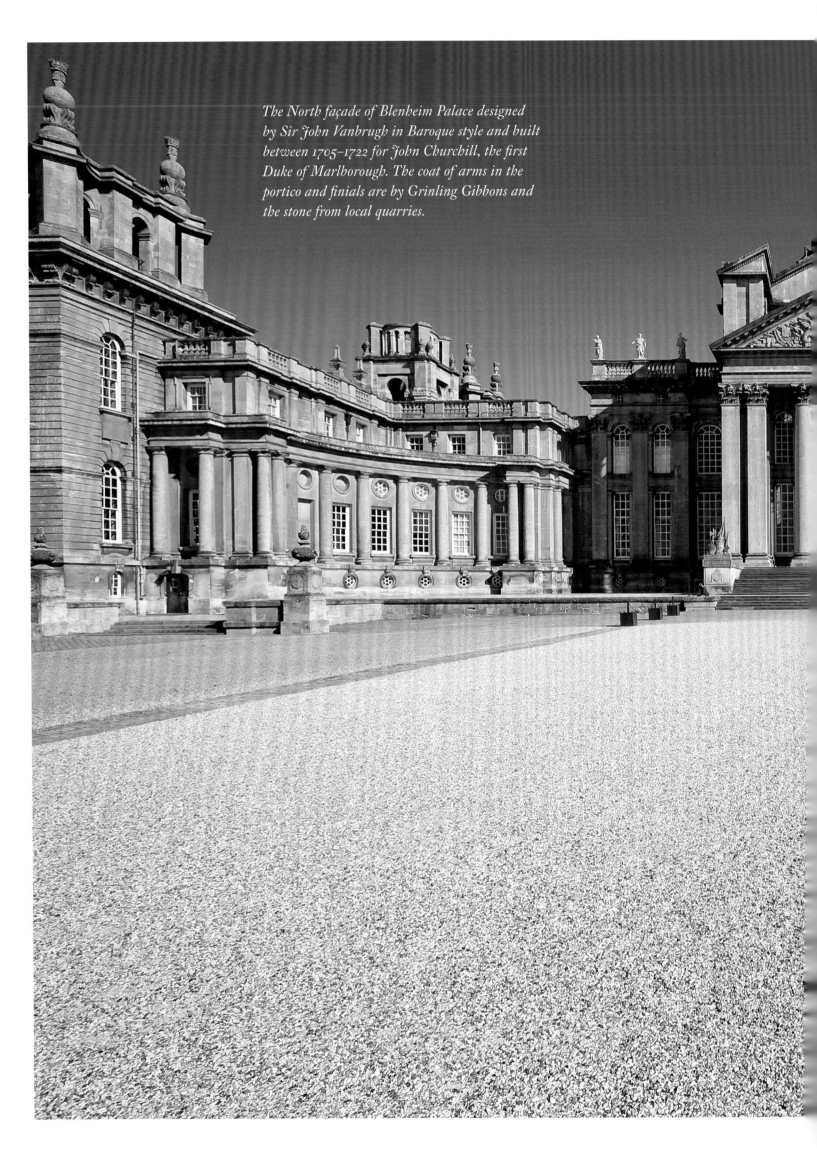

The North façade of Blenheim Palace designed
by Sir John Vanbrugh in Baroque style and built
between 1705–1722 for John Churchill, the first
Duke of Marlborough. The coat of arms in the
portico and finials are by Grinling Gibbons and
the stone from local quarries.

IN the early seventeenth century a great deal of Jacobean manor houses were built with an emphasis on symmetry and uniformity – in particular of exterior façades and the placement of windows and chimney stacks. Inigo Jones, who had travelled extensively to Italy in the early sixteenth century, was the main influence in transforming English architecture and spreading the message of the classical disciplines of order, scale and proportion. Initially this was reserved for the grandest of houses, with Jones acting as surveyor general to the king's works, but soon his influence and that of Andrea Palladio and the Classical architects' bible, *I Quattro Libri dell'Architettura*, spread to smaller houses, creating the simple box-like house with evenly placed windows, a central front door, sloping pitched roof with plain chimneys rising from it that is so pleasingly familiar to us today. In many areas, the transformation to classical simplicity was halted by influences from the Low Countries, such as Dutch curved gables and a variety of shapes and styles of windows, which persisted in many merchants' houses in areas where rebuilding was less frequent and houses were handed from father to son. As a result of the popularity of symmetrical and even exteriors, the layout of interiors became much more harmonious, resulting in increased light, deliberate placement of doors and fireplaces and an orderly framework of architectural ornamentation and panelling.

Baroque style, which had originated in Rome in about 1620, reached England around 1670. It was a very opulent style designed to impress and surprise and show drama. As it was not suited to small houses, the extravagance and complexity of Baroque craftsmanship was reserved for large stately homes that could afford and manage the style: houses such as Chatsworth, Petworth and Blenheim, which are testament to the skills of great craftsmen such as Grinling Gibbons and artists such as Antonio Verrio and Louis Laguerre.

CHIMNEY STACKS

The invention of the chimney led to control of heat and light and less smoke wafting around the roof space. Chimneys became a necessity, once coal replaced wood as the principle source of heat. The wealthy could afford more than one chimney, making chimney stacks status symbols. In Tudor times, red brickwork was highly fashionable and expensive, and of course a great material for building ornate chimney stacks. Revenue collectors saw chimneys proudly sprouting on rooftops and came up with a very unpopular hearth tax, which in turn led to alterations in home design, with multiple flues snaking through the walls to join one central stack.

The roofscape at Blenheim gives an insight into the complexity of Vanbrugh's design for the house – in the 17th and 18th centuries, fireplaces were the only form of heating. The carvings on the towers are by Grinling Gibbons.

Nicholas Hawksmoor designed this glorious Baroque house, Easton Neston in Northamptonshire, in 1694 for Sir William Fermor. The red brick building to the side was part of an earlier house designed by Christopher Wren.

FOLLOWING the death of Queen Anne in 1714 and the arrival of the Hanoverian Georges, the short-lived Baroque style, associated with the authoritarian rule of the Stuarts, fell out of favour. There was a desire to move away from the excesses of Baroque, and the short reign of Queen Anne allowed for a cooling-off period, leading to simple, elegant taste, clean lines and more comfort. This led the way to Palladianism – an architectural style with emphasis on Classical detail, scale and proportion – championed by Lord Burlington, Thomas Coke and William Kent with the initial design principles inspired by the publication of Colen Campbell's *Vitruvius Britannicus*. This group continued to revive the style and principles of the Classical orders which Inigo Jones had started the previous century, referencing the works of Palladio which were paramount. It was a demanding style – nothing was left to chance, and entire rooms were designed from walls and ceilings and floors and down to the furniture.

Façades were simple and symmetrical with low-pitched roofs partially screened by parapets. Many houses had a centre section with a large pediment or portico with wings flanking the main section.

Towards the mid part of the century, there was a movement away from the constraints of Palladianism, and with influences from France and the Rococo style, a more lighted-hearted, whimsical, asymmetrical style incorporating Gothic Revival and Chinoiserie was established, best epitomised in Horace Walpole's Strawberry Hill. It was, however, on the interior that Rococo style became more established, with arched doors, windows and panels; rounded corners; elaborated, coved ceilings richly decorated, with C- and S-shaped scrolls, shells, ribbons and flowers in abundance being quite the norm.

Early eighteenth-century designs were inspired by the pattern books published by men such as Batty Langley, Isaac Ware and William Halfpenny, leading to the *Rule of Taste*, a publication which spread to the country builder and craftsman. Many designs were similar to those already established by Inigo Jones but were now finding their way into more modest houses.

top left *This charming 17th-Century stone farmhouse in Cumbria was bought by Beatrix Potter in 1905, and the interiors inspired many of her writings.*

top right *A la Ronde, near Exmouth, was built in the 18th Century by Jane and Mary Parminter and inspired by their travels in Europe. It has sixteen sides, and it is believed the design was based on the Basilica of San Vitale in Rome.*

right *Starting out as a modest cottage in Twickenham, Strawberry Hill was transformed between 1749 and 1776 by Horace Walpole into the finest example of Georgian Gothic Revival architecture.*

FOLLOWING the boom of building work during the first half of the eighteenth century, the second half concentrated more on additions or changing the internal decoration. The leading architects and designers of this Neo-Classical period were Robert Adam and his brother James, Henry Holland, James Wyatt and William Chambers. Influenced by Classical Roman and Greek buildings and the discoveries of arabesque decoration at Herculaneum and Pompeii, Robert Adam set about transforming interiors with an array of characteristic ornaments such as swags, urns, scrolls, husks, arabesques, garlands, etc., and using them in a much lighter fashion than previously seen. In his buildings, he worked closely with the plasterer Joseph Rose to create masterpieces such as Syon House, Osterley and Kedleston, using a variety of geometric shapes for not only the shape of the rooms but for floors and ceiling patterns, too. Adam designed the entire room including fireplaces, furniture and carpets with the same Classical motifs used on painted pieces, as inlay and for carpet designs woven by Axminster or Wilton to reflect the design of the ceiling.

Apart from Adam's work there was great deal of superior craftsmanship being carried out at the same time, and the works of Thomas Sheraton and Thomas Chippendale were being widely spread through pattern books. This, along with an increased choice of building materials, led the way for the rising middle classes to learn and replicate the designs in the new villas being built across the country, resulting in a huge number of exquisitely crafted new homes.

The style of the late eighteenth-century house became less formal and more relaxed with the advent of the Picturesque movement, which allowed for house and garden to harmonize within the landscape. More formal rooms were built onto the back of the house, with French windows leading out onto the terrace and gardens designed to please by the likes of Humphrey Repton and Richard Payne Knight. Additions to houses, such as conservatories and breakfast rooms, led to façades becoming asymmetrical and the terrace becoming part of the living space.

Town houses, too, became less uniform with a range of new techniques and building materials, allowing brick, stone and stucco houses to sit side by side.

By the end of the eighteenth century, there was a move away from the intricate detail of the Neo-Classical period to the fresher, simpler and lighter style of the Regency period, so called after the Prince Regent, George III, who had established his own style by the alteration of his London residence at Carlton House. Architects such as Nash, Wyatt and Soane were keen to return to the more sober influence of the Renaissance period, when interiors were plainer with less ornament and simpler architectural details. They, too, left their mark, taking their influence from India, in the case of Nash's Brighton Pavilion, as well as Greece and Italy which influenced the Classical style of new grand city terraces such as in Bath and London's Regents Park. Their brick façades with long, tall sash windows with pediments in contrasting stone typified the elegance of the period.

This early Queen Anne terrace house in London dates from 1708 and was the home of Thomas Carlyle, satirical writer and essayist, and his wife Jane from 1834. The layout is typical of the period with the kitchen in the basement, parlour on the ground floor, drawing room on the first floor and bedrooms above.

This unique fantasy house, Plas Newydd, was the home of the Ladies of Llangollen, Lady Eleanor Butler and Miss Sarah Ponsonby. Their notorious relationship scandalised Regency society, and their home became a meeting place for artists, writers and other "outsiders". They transformed the original modest cottage into a romantic Gothicized mansion between 1798 and 1819 by adding elaborate stained-glass windows, plasterwork and the carved oak panels.

Built by James Gibbs in 1722 for the 2nd Earl of Litchfield, the façade of this Palladian house is typical of the early Georgian period. It is built from local stone with an eleven-bay centre section and curved corridors that connect to separate wings with cupolas.

"Ah, to build, to build! That is the noblest art of all the arts. Painting and sculpture are but images, are merely shadows cast by outward things on stone or canvas, having in themselves no separate existence. Architecture, existing in itself, and not in seeming a something it is not, surpasses them as substance shadow."

Henry Wadsworth Longfellow (1807–1882) American poet

> "Light, God's eldest daughter, is a principal beauty in a building."
>
> Thomas Fuller (1823–1898)
> Canadian architect

TECHNOLOGY LEAPS FORWARD

In medieval times, "wind eyes" were holes in the wall that let in the light and were closed against intruders and inclement weather with shutters. Flat glass for windows was rare during the 17th Century; panes of blown glass were small, dimpled and full of air bubbles. In the 18th Century, moulded glass was a technical leap forward, and by the 19th Century, machinery for floating, polishing and grinding glass were on the way to producing an affordable architectural material, making life more convenient, safe and comfortable for all. Modern technology puts glass in the frame as a sustainable, versatile building material. It can be used for walls, floors and ceilings to dramatic effect.

DAYLIGHT ROBBERY

Window tax was first levied in 1696 to help fund William III's expensive conflicts in Ireland and France. It replaced the unpopular Hearth Tax, which had tax collectors muscling their way into homes and counting fireplaces. A window tax, it was argued, could be enforced from the outside and was fair because the rich would pay more. Up to 6 windows was free, 7 to 9 windows two shillings, 10 to 19 four shillings, over 20 eight shillings. People got round this unpopular tax on light and air by blocking up windows, but not all blocked-up windows are tax dodges – some were built that way to add symmetry to the outside of a building. The tax, described by a campaigning Member of Parliament as having made "the government hateful to the eyes of the people", was repealed in 1851.

THE Victorian period saw a huge change in the architecture and decoration of houses, largely due to a wealthy society whose desire was to show off their wealth to the detriment of taste and style. It was the lure of the past that led the cacophony of style: Neo-Rococo, Gothic, Neo-Jacobean, Scottish Baronial, Moorish, Tudor and Ecclesiastical were often unwisely intermingled. Thanks to the railway and an abundance of building materials, there was a building boom and new town houses were built, forming new suburbs in existing towns and cities. The typical terraced house had four floors with basement and attic and a staircase to one side of the house. The basement housed the kitchen and servants' quarters, the ground floor the dining room and parlour. On the first floor was the main drawing room and on upper floors, the bedrooms. Bathrooms did not exist as a separate room until after the 1870s.

Max Gate in Dorset is a lovely Victorian villa, designed by the writer Thomas Hardy and built by his brother in 1885.

Houses were solidly built with high, ornate ceilings, elaborate plaster details, heavy wood panelling and wood or encaustic tiled floors. Some of the cacophonous styles were replicated as authentically as possible using antique salvaged materials such as stained glass and panelling, and in America it was fashionable to transport entire rooms from Europe. Other houses looked to different styles for different rooms, the library and hall typically showing elements of Gothic, whilst drawing rooms and bedrooms were more feminine, with Rococo curves and swirls.

As mass production led to an increasing plethora of Victorian styles, towards the end of the century there was an inevitable movement away from the ornate Gothic and Ecclesiastical buildings favoured by Pugin towards simplicity and good craftsmanship pioneered by the Aesthetic movement, led by the likes of William Morris and Voysey as well as architects Ashbee and Lethaby. Morris's own company produced furniture, stained glass, wallpaper, textiles and pottery, and his aim was to not only produce high-quality goods but make them available to all. In reality, his own designs were expensive, but his style was copied by many manufacturers and made affordable to the middle classes.

The writer Charles Eastlake published his book *Hints on Household Taste* in 1868. His theory was that houses should evolve gradually with passion and quality. Eastlake favoured the Queen Anne style: comfort, quality and informality with houses built in red brick with a simple asymmetrical form, bow and sash windows and rooms of a manageable size. The period following the excess of High Victorian, the more simplified Arts and Crafts and the Queen Anne style was a rather inconsequential style known as Edwardian. Houses were more substantial and less fussy, with architectural elements taken from previous periods but simplified. Staircases had plain square balusters, windows were either sash or casement, and walls had simple panelling or a paint finish. The largest change to the interior was the introduction of electric lighting, which led to brighter pastel shades of paint with a glossy finish. Wallpaper was delicate with a French influence or naturalistic flowers and foliage. All was pleasant enough, but what was needed now was a big leap forwards.

left *This suburban house in Priory Gardens, Bedford Park, in West London, is noted as one of the earliest examples of a garden suburb. It was initiated by Jonathan Carr, cloth merchant and property speculator, and the development proved to be influential all over the world. It was built in the 1880s, and many of the houses are in the Queen Anne style designed by noted architect William Norman Shaw.*

opposite *Another Bedford Park house designed by the architect Edward John May, who was brought in by Shaw to assist with the development. The red Suffolk brick combined with stucco and Brosely roof tiles and white paint are all part of the overall village design.*

left *Originally built in 1780 by Winslow Crocker, this house was moved in 1936 by Mary Thacher, and meticulously taken apart and rebuilt to form a backdrop for her collection of historic furniture and objects. It is a great example of a typical Colonial Cape Cod house.*

below left *A typical example of a New Orleans Garden District house built in the mid 18th Century in the Greek Revival style, with Ionic columns and wrought-iron balustrade on the first-floor terrace.*

opposite *Millford Plantation in South Carolina is an exquisite example of a Greek Revival plantation house built in 1839 for John L. Manning, the governor of South Carolina by the architect Nathanial F. Potter. The portico is supported by granite columns with Corinthian capitals.*

"I would have, then, our ordinary dwelling-houses built to last, and built to be lovely; as rich and full of pleasantness as may be within and without … with such differences as might suit and express each man's character and occupation, and partly his history."

John Ruskin (1819–1900)
English art critic and social thinker

FOLLOWING the end of the First World War and advances in technology (electricity and in-house plumbing) and construction methods, there was a huge push for architects to move forward and develop their own style using new techniques and materials such as steel, concrete and plate glass. Most of the successful postwar architects emanated from Germany, where the Bauhaus movement was influential in spreading the International style. Emphasis was placed on simplicity, clean lines and lack of detail, open-plan layouts, and quality materials. As the International style developed in Europe, Frank Lloyd Wright was developing Modernism in America. His Prairie style concentrated on the view to the outside from within, contrasting natural materials and textures such as brick juxtaposed against plain white plaster or an entire wall of glass. Internal layouts were open plan, with large focal points such as a large fireplace. Whilst architects continued the struggle to develop a major new style, some notable interior designers were making their mark. Many of the landed gentry and wealthy English had no desire to change the way they lived or decorated their houses and indeed it would have been unsuitable. Old houses were restored and updated to take into account the new reality and life without servants. In London, Syrie Maugham was using a lot of glass and various tones of white, and her success soon spread into America. Her signature was limewashed walls and French furniture painted in natural colours of crackle paint. The famous decorator Nancy Lancaster joined the firm of Colefax and Fowler after the war and set about transforming her own houses, Kelmash and Ditchley, and assisting the legendary John Fowler, who not only had extraordinary talent for seeing how a house should work architecturally, but also a wonderful sense of colour and comfort, ensuring rooms flowed and were used for their intended purpose.

BUILDING UTOPIA

Le Corbusier, the "father of modern architecture" famously decreed that houses were "machines for living in." His *Unité d'Habitation* in Firminy, a mining community in Central France, opened in the mid-1960s. It was one example of his utopian dream of a vertical community for working people with an onsite school, "streets" in the sky, apartments flooded with sunlight and views over parkland. Central to his vision was the woman at home preparing food, the man of the house and children returning at the end of the day to gather round the 'hearth' of the home, although there was no hearth and the kitchen area was only 10 feet square. The flats were small and offered little privacy for real-life families and even less storage space. (Corbusier had no children of his own, and his wife Yvonne was no cook.) Some people loved them, but most soon moved out to the more ramshackle, less didactic spaces they were used to. Some of the apartments in this *Unité d'Habitation* are still used for social housing, the remaining flats are privately owned *pieds-à-terre*.

previous pages *This modernist home – The Homewood – was designed by architect Patrick Gwynne for his parents in 1938 when he was just 24. His influences were Le Corbusier and Miles van der Rohe. It has clean lines and open-plan living spaces. The grounds were designed to fit in with the house.*

above *Designed by students of the Frank Lloyd Wright School of Architecture at Taliesin, this Mod Fab prototype home is built to be transportable by road. It runs entirely on green technology.*

right *An Earthship in Taos, New Mexico, based on the work of Michael Reynolds and built according to his Biotecture method which uses only natural and recycled materials. The charming, quirky homes are totally sustainable buildings that naturally regulate internal temperatures and rely on energy from the sun and water from rain, snow and condensation.*

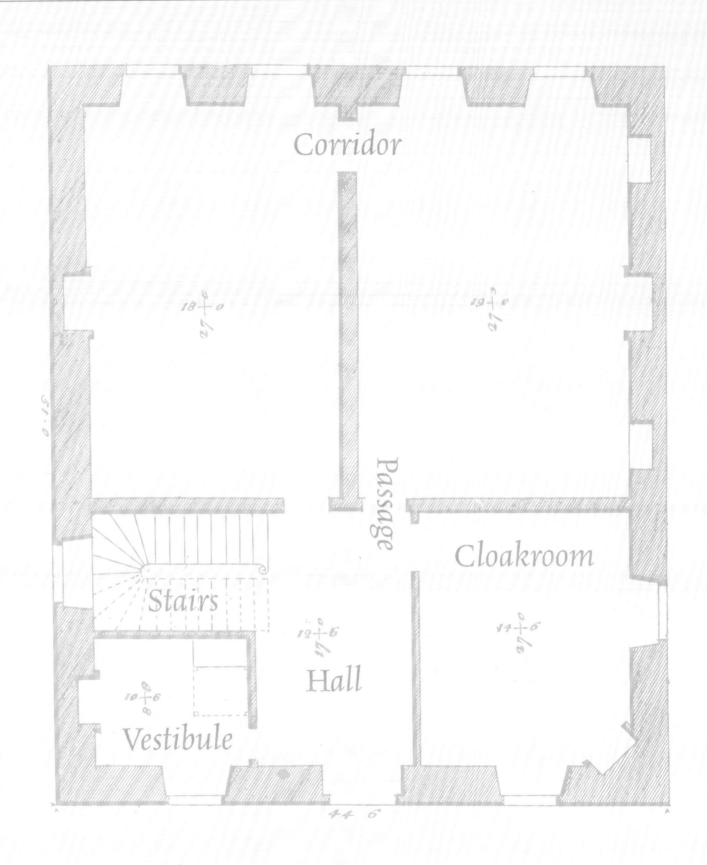

Corridor

Passage

18+0 / 27+6

29+6 / 27+6

15.0

Stairs

Cloakroom

14+6 / 27+0

12+6 / 17+6

Hall

10+6 / 8+8

Vestibule

44 6

HALLS

UNTIL the mid-sixteenth century, the hall was often the only room in the house, other than a servants' kitchen and possibly a Great Chamber or Solar for the lord of the manor. Early halls were laid out in the manner of a church or barn but with a central fire or brazier that was far from practical, as it needed open louvers in the rafters to allow smoke to escape. The entire household congregated and ate and slept in the hall, with the family being isolated to one end often on a raised dais: "Knight, and page and household squire, loitered through the loft hall, or crowded round the ample fire."

The wall fireplace with projecting stone hood dates from about the thirteenth century, which in turn led to walls being decorated firstly with whitewash and then a form of thin plaster which could be painted with heraldic emblems. Simple wainscot panelling was introduced in the grander homes and royal palaces and reportedly painted. Wall hangings and tapestries were welcome additions for insulation from about the fourteenth century, with a decorative (and draught-excluding) canopy over the chair of the lord of the manor. By the fifteenth and sixteenth centuries, many halls had windows, typically on one side only, and one or two wall fireplaces and, although still the principal room, there were a series of separate rooms for servants and family leading off it. Often these rooms were on different stories with either a simple internal wood staircase to gain access or, more commonly, an external stone one. Windows became larger, often with a central bay with a built-in seat, and the structure of the wood beams and panelling became more complex incorporating carvings. Whilst meals still took place in the Great Hall, a desire for more privacy and comfort was met first with screens and then, as new houses were built for pleasure rather than as fortresses, separate parlours were provided where the family could eat and retire to and the communal hall became obsolete. New houses now had a small vestibule with a low plastered ceiling, where guests would wait before being ushered into other living rooms.

Carried out in 1726, this sumptuous plasterwork in the Saloon at Ditchley Park, is by Adalbertus Artari and Francesco Serena. It depicts a combination of early Georgian and Rococo motifs with fluted pilasters and scrolls and shells. The walls were originally green and are now marbleized in a sienna colour.

left *Details of the plasterwork and a coloured visual by Alexandre Serebrikoff, commissioned by Marietta Tree as a gift to her husband Ronald as a memento to their time at Ditchley in the 1930s and '40s.*

opposite *The fireplace in the Great Hall created under the direction of William Kent. The portrait is of the 2nd Earl of Litchfield, for whom the house was built.*

FIDE ET CONSTANTIA

THE GENTLEMANLY HANG

The most fashionable way to hang a collection of paintings in the late eighteenth century was known as the Gentlemanly Hang, which reflected the art education of the European aristocrat largely gained during the Grand Tour. A Gentlemanly Hang was like an art history lesson displaying 16th- and 17th-Century Italian, Flemish, Dutch and French old masters in a way that highlighted and contrasted their formal qualities, such as composition and chiaroscuro, and might feature, for instance, a French Venus contrasted with a Flemish Venus or an Italian martyr and a Dutch martyr. Gradually tastes shifted away from decorating the walls with evidence of an education in favour of more contemporary works. Family portraits, once so posed and heroic and swathed in mythology, became far more lifelike and revealing of true character.

above *The 4th Duke and Duchess of Marlborough and their children painted by Sir Joshua Reynolds in 1778, one of the favoured artists of the time.*

right *A coloured visual of the Great Hall at Ditchley by Alexandre Serebrikoff which was painted in the 1930s. Little has changed.*

"The job of buildings is to improve human relations: architecture must ease them, not make them worse."

Ralph Erskine (1914–2005) British-born architect

above *The Octagon Hall at A la Ronde which is 35 feet high and off which all main rooms radiate. The house was built by spinster cousins following their Grand Tour in Europe.*

opposite *The central Great Hall at Breakers, a summer home in Newport designed for Cornelius Vanderbilt II by Richard Hunt in 1893. All rooms are arranged symmetrically around this impressive 50-foot-square and 50-foot-high entrance.*

HALLS, galleries, corridors and staircases now became a means of moving visitors, family and servants around the house as befitted their status. The central position of the hall was important, not just for establishing favourable first impressions and allowing access, but for filtering light throughout the house.

By the early seventeenth century, open well staircases, which superseded the modest practical straight flights hidden behind walls or turrets, were leading off the vestibule to the first floor where bedrooms were now located. By the Baroque era, the staircase had become a main architectural feature that led off the main hall or vestibule, sweeping guests up to the first floor, where the principal rooms were housed. The floor of the hall was either in a local stone or wood plank and meant to impress, as first impressions were important. The fireplace was the focal point and walls were panelled either half height or full height and the ceiling and cornice were fashioned in decorative plasterwork. Furniture was sparse as it was a merely a place to wait.

Throughout the eighteenth century the layout of the hall and the importance of the staircase changed little except that details became more refined with the style of the plasterwork relevant to the style and period of the house. Staircases now extended to upper floors and may have had a skylight with oval or round dome or flat glass panel allowing light to filter down the well. Some grander homes had a double staircase – starting with one main flight and branching out on either side to reach a first floor gallery. These open galleries allowed additional light to flow down from upper windows, connecting the two principal floors.

The Garden Hall at Easton Neston leads off the main hall and staircase and the full-length window provides views east over the landscaped gardens and Long Water, also designed by the architect Nicholas Hawksmoor. The gilded pelmet was made recently, specifically for the window. The walls are covered with a moiré fabric, and the ceiling is the original groin vault.

Originally one room with the adjacent drawing room, this hall, which was designed by Nicolas Hawksmoor, has recently been renovated. The marble fireplace was added as well as the door to the left, which provides access to the rear hall. The stone floors are original 18th Century, and the tapestry is authentic to that period.

left *View from the hall to the staircase vestibule showing the original Corinthian stone columns and niches. A niche opposite the foot of the main stairs now houses a later statue.*

centre *The benches are copies of a design by William Kent made specifically for the Garden Hall. The Dutch landscapes work well for the period of the house. The original dark frames were replaced by lighter gilt ones.*

right *Originally a series of small-portioned rooms housing wc's, the space was cold and uninviting. By installing old panelling to match some existing ones, it has been transformed into an elegant back hall.*

following pages *Typical of many English houses since the Baroque period is an enfilade of rooms along one axis of the house which allows for good circulation when entertaining.*

opposite *A very grand hall at Marble House in Newport, with rooms and corridors leading off it. Designed by Richard Hunt for William Kissam Vanderbilt in the Gilded Age between 1888 and 1892, it was said to be influenced by Le Petit Trianon at Versailles.*

above *An enfilade of bedrooms at Blenheim, whereby each room has a door with space in between which can be conveniently used as a wardrobe. Originally the adjacent room would have been a dressing room or sitting room (great chamber).*

left *View through an enfilade of bedrooms at the early 18th-Century Mompesson House in Wiltshire, showing a nice contrast between the painted panelling and woodwork and solid eight-panelled mahogany doors.*

B Y Victorian times, many terraced houses were being built, and this meant the hall was reduced in size and the staircase, although still fairly substantial, was set against the main retaining wall in a straight run up to a half landing or the next floor. Treads on the main floors were either wood or stone, with the bottom step being larger and rounded with a large newel post. Large wrought-iron or machine-turned wood balusters were typical but the higher you went, the simpler the baluster. In country houses, the Victorian staircase was still an important focal point, with walls decorated with dado-height panelling and wallpaper or paint above. Floors were laid with either encaustic tiles or wood planking with decorative rugs.

Although halls were still sparsely furnished, the Victorian hall gave a feeling of warmth and welcome with warm, strong colours such as red and green, and windows dressed with heavy velvets. A mirror over an open fireplace helped to reflect light, and walls were usually hung with pictures or perhaps taxidermy in glass cases. There was usually some element of uphol-stery – a wing chair or buttoned sofa with lavish trim-mings – and a large gas-fuelled chandelier or exotic lamp and shade. The introduction of electricity and heating added to the sense of welcome.

This corridor or loggia was purpose-built to provide the connection between an existing farmhouse and an adjacent barn. It looks over the courtyard and gives the impression of having originally been open on one side which traditionally it would have been.

opposite, clockwise from top left *This new corridor was created in an existing wing of the house following a new internal layout. The groin vault ceiling adds architectural detail and the stone floor is laid in panels to reflect the ceiling. A rib-vaulted ceiling is in the Gothic style with cherry wood emphasising the ribs and forming Gothic columns. A new linking corridor in a home with Tudor origins and 18th- and* 19th-*Century additions. A fan-vaulted papier-mâché ceiling at Strawberry Hill – a fine example of Georgian Gothic architecture.*

below *This groin vault ceiling is in a new-build Georgian style home in the United States, and the plasterwork relief is in the Neo-Classical style. It was typical at the time to paint the ceiling in soft pastel colours and leave the relief in white.*

THE back hall or, as it is more often known, the boot room or cloakroom, is a typical feature of many a country house and an invaluable addition to the practical functioning of a home. Located now where the servants' or tradesman's entrance once was, often conveniently next to the kitchen or pantry, this is usually used in modern-day life by the family on a regular basis. It is a place to store boots, coats, prams and bicycles, a place for dogs to sleep and a general dumping ground for 'stuff'. In grander homes the boot room may have been on a lower level, in the undercroft or basement with a robust flagstone floor and simple whitewashed walls.

Snaking though the house away from the main staircase, the grander homes installed a secondary concealed staircase, mainly for use by servants, but also often the only means by which to reach the attic or basement levels. A series of passages led off the back stairs' landings, giving access to the main rooms through doors concealed in the panelling, so servants could magically appear and disappear without having to make an entrance or an exit.

This original 18th-Century panelled room provides an elegant boot and gunroom. The oak floor and fireplace are original, and the walls were recently repainted.

left Entrance to the boot room on the previous page. It has been treated as an elegant 18th-Century room, with curtains to add warmth. The jib door conceals a cupboard.

above This original oak staircase dates from the 16th Century and is made from blocks of oak with simple square balusters, newel post and handrail. At this time, newel posts were purely functional and not an important architectural feature.

BLENHEIM STAIRS

The back stairs at Blenheim Palace led down into the basement kitchens and up to the staff sleeping accommodation in the attic rooms tucked above the main bedroom floor. Known as Housemaid's Heights, most of these small rooms had a little fireplace and some natural daylight filtering through from a skylight or a floor-level window, but the hard-working servants probably spent little time in their rooms other than sleeping. The staircase itself is simple but substantial and is hidden away from general view behind grand mahogany doors. The original house bells, connected via a bell pull to most of the major rooms in the house, are still in evidence outside the kitchen; they are the external evidence of a complex and ingenious interior mechanical network of wires and pulleys. Before the advent of the bell pull, servants were obliged to hover in corridors and hallways, awaiting a shouted summons.

THE fashion for secular, pictorial stained glass and lead lights was largely Victorian. Coloured glass was a popular addition to front doors and stairwell windows, as it allowed light to stream through colour, adding drama and warmth to what was often a dark, restricted space.

Terraced town houses, in particular, pose a challenge in creating a practical and welcoming area with no space to play with and no particular architectural feature to emphasize. In many cases, this problem is solved not just by windows and lighting but by adding double doors to an adjacent room and opening up the hall to the dining room or living room. Where possible, halls, corridors or landings should be treated like the rooms they once were. If there is no space for furniture, wallpaper and pictures will help to humanise the space.

In many modernist and contemporary houses the emphasis is still as it always was – to ensure that the staircase and hall are seen as strategic areas of the house, creating a striking first impression. With sophisticated technology and building materials, some staircases have become more like a piece of sculpture, literally floating in the space with glass or wood treads and glass or metal balusters. Clever lighting installed in the wall or on individual treads can transform a practical entrance hall into a place of beauty.

An Arts and Crafts/Gothic Revival stained-glass window and a little Gothic window with modern stained glass at Strawberry Hill provide wonderful focal points and allow interesting lights shafts to fall on the polished wood surfaces.

above *The entrance hall of a modernist house designed by Erno Goldfinger in 1938 shows an opaque glass wall with shelves displaying coloured glass, a novel way to introduce changing colours of light.*

opposite top *The modest entrance and staircase in John Lennon's childhood Liverpool home show a good example of stained glass of the time.*

opposite *The entrance of an Earthship house made from recycled materials, including glass bottles which make a colourful light play around the front door.*

"Space and light and order. Those are the things that men need just as much as they need bread or a place to sleep.

Charles Edouard Jeanneret (Le Corbusier) (1887–1965)
Swiss-born modernist architect

SHOWCASE FOR A STAIRCASE

Medieval castles had spiral stairs
so that defenders, descending, had their right
sword arms free and attackers, ascending,
found themselves at a distinct disadvantage.
In more peaceful and prosperous times,
staircases were built to impress visitors and
sweep them onwards and upwards to the
grandest rooms situated on the first floor.
For architects and craftsmen, a staircase
represented a grand opportunity to show off
their skills: the cantilever, the balustrades, the
plasterwork and ornamentation, all of which
could be admired from so many angles in
massive full-height stairwells. The restrained
sensitivities of the Georgian era led to straight
flights of steps with a lower flight, a half
landing and an upper flight so that stairs could
be built into houses rather than rooms
taking their position around
the stairwell.

previous pages *This magnificent stone staircase and wrought-iron balustrade was designed by Nicholas Hawksmoor in the style of Jean Tijou, and the painted grisailles are by Sir James Thornhill. The 48-light chandelier is a copy of the original and made from rock crystal and cast brass with each leaf hand-crafted in brass.*

above *This oval staircase was recently designed and built in a new-build house in Dallas, Texas. The combination of metal and wood balusters is reminiscent of an 18th-Century design.*

right *The simple modernist spiral stairs at Homewood House, designed in 1938, are made from concrete with a terrazzo finish. The large sunken uplighter adds to the effect.*

left *This staircase at Millford Plantation in South Carolina is encased in a domed rotunda and leads off the main hall, forming the centerpiece of the house. The style of the house is Greek Revival and the features are typical of that period.*

above *This floating staircase was designed by architect Bill Baker and myself and is in a new-build house in Atlanta. The structure is supported by a steel frame and then encased to make it look like a sculpture. The balusters are in wrought iron and handrail is mahogany.*

far left *A different view of the elegant oval staircase shown on the previous page. The walls are in a polished plaster finish, the floor is limestone, and the treads and risors are in wood. The lit niches are perfect for the display of sculptures.*

left *A striking new-build oak staircase which was part of the remodeling of a 17th-Century house. The subtle custom-made stained-glass window helps block a dull view and uses elements from the family crest, adding a touch of the history of the building and the family.*

bottom left and right *Built in an old barn, this modern staircase is like a piece of sculpture and can provide access from the ground floor to the upper gallery, where there is a library. In reality, it is not used, as there is another staircase, but it does make a great focal point.*

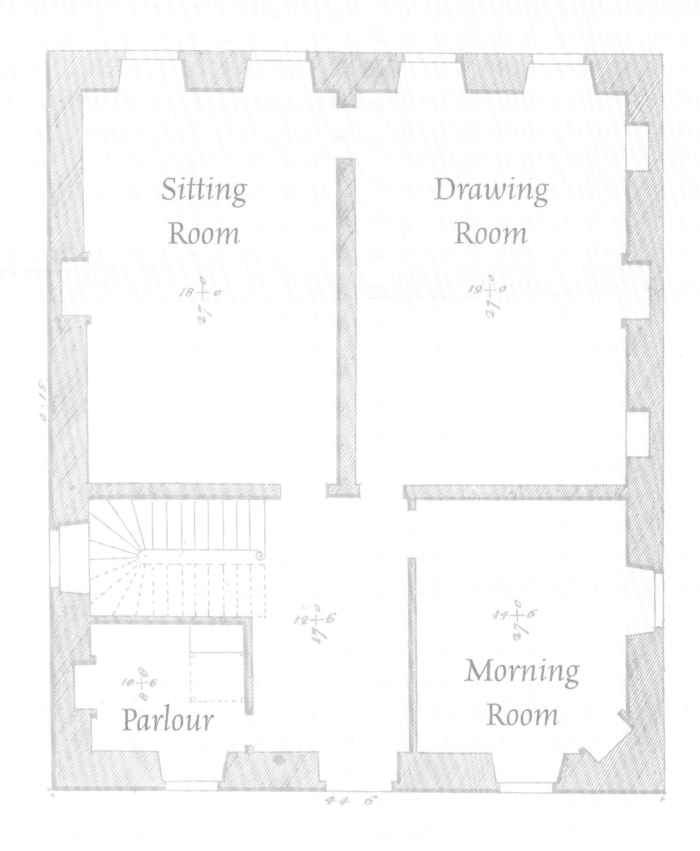

LIVING ROOMS

THE concept of a living room did not really come into being until the sixteenth century. In the medieval Great Hall, the parlour, a place for the family to sleep, greet guests and relax away from the general household hubbub, was placed at one end of the hall behind the dais. As separate rooms for sleeping were introduced, the parlour situated on the ground floor next to the kitchen served principally as an eating room. It was generally panelled, inviting and warm and often known as the winter parlour. Some larger houses had a series of parlours, one on the ground floor for eating and one on the first floor for family gatherings. In the grandest of houses there was yet another parlour reserved for the upper servants to take their meals.

In the early sixteenth century, the plan of the house changed dramatically. Many of the new styles of H-type and courtyard houses have layouts that include a withdrawing room and a long gallery as well as the parlour, with the family rooms placed on one side of the vestibule and the servants' rooms on the other.

The long gallery was a typical feature of Elizabethan houses and used for entertaining guests, as a music room or to partake of indoor exercise in winter months. Walls were generally panelled and hung with tapestries and embroideries; ceilings were panelled or adorned with strapwork plasterwork. Furniture, consisting of upright chairs and court cupboards, was placed around the perimeter – these rooms were not designed for comfort.

The term "withdrawing room" or "chamber" was first applied to a small room adjacent to the main chamber, which subsequently became the main sitting room – a private room where the master of the house may take supper or retire to after meals.

By the seventeenth century, the drawing room had become more accessible. It was a room to invite guests and primarily where the ladies withdrew to take tea, play cards and sew. In grander houses, the French fashion for the *salon* saw the creation of a room for grand entertaining and banqueting which was often double height with a domed ceiling. In the Victorian period some *grand salons*, such as the one at Blenheim, were turned into sitting rooms.

this page and previous page The drawing room at Easton Neston was originally a triple-story Great Hall that stretched to the south wall and resembled a medieval hall. In the 19th Century, the plan was changed to create a double height, and a partition wall (facing in the picture) was erected to make the room a more manageable space. The current furnishings have been recently added for the present owner.

DURING the early eighteenth century, many houses were remodelled to embrace new lifestyles and entertaining. The main living rooms were on the ground floor and the servants' quarters were removed to basement level or the attics, as was the case at Blenheim. To add new formal entertaining rooms to an existing house often involved creating a completely new wing, such as at Chatsworth, where an enfilade of salon and antechambers were added.

By the eighteenth century, decoration became less formal and rooms more comfortable. The fireplace was a main focal point in all living rooms, and decorative panelling, plasterwork ceilings and cornices were not just reserved for grand houses but new villas and manor houses, too. The style and lavishness of the decor was dictated by wealth as well as availability. Many fabrics such as silk and taffeta were expensive, but from the Rococo period onwards, wallpapers and cotton fabrics were printed and produced more cheaply and it became more affordable to dress walls and windows and change upholstery.

Neo-Classical architects, such as Robert Adam, designed entire rooms from the architectural details to the furniture, carpets and soft furnishings, and in this way living rooms became more comfortable, personal and inviting. By the Regency period, informality and comfort were key components, with furniture now placed around the fireplace or in companionable groups. Conservatories with French doors leading onto the garden were added onto existing houses, providing an additional summer reception room. As a result of this, and the increasing use of the library as a family living room, the drawing room became reserved for formal entertaining. In some later additions, the living room and drawing rooms may have been combined with double doors between to allow for one larger room when required.

previous page *This smoking room is in Dennis Severs' Georgian terraced house in Spitalfields, London, and dates from 1724. The wood panelling is original and the room is furnished and propped to give the impression of life at that time, as if the owner has just stepped out of the room.*

above *The parlour at Batemans, a 17th-Century Jacobean house which was home to the writer Rudyard Kipling from 1902 to 1936. The oak beams, oak panelling and stone mullioned windows are typical of the period but the furnishings are 19th and 20th Century. The velvet Knole sofa is typical of the style of early furniture.*

"Home is a name, a word,
it is a strong one; stronger than
magician ever spoke, or spirit
ever answered to."

Charles Dickens (1812–1870)
British novelist

above The parlour at Hilltop, where Beatrix Potter
lived and wrote, has 18th-Century wood panelling
and a marble Adam-style fireplace. The walls are
adorned with silhouettes and a Regency convex
mirror, and the lighting is a mix of candlelight and
gas lamps.

As travel became easier in the eighteenth century, entertaining at home was more popular and guests were often invited not just to dinner but dinner and dancing, too. Having taken dinner in the salon or dining room, guests would withdraw to the drawing room to play cards, drink tea or listen to music before returning to the salon for dancing.

Tea drinking was highly fashionable and, for this purpose, specialist tea tables were made with a fretwork gallery or a piecrust-shaped top that had a lip to stop china falling off. Tea was stored in decorative tea caddies and some of these were used into a type of worktable called a teapoy, incorporating a couple of wooden boxes and maybe a glass dish for sugar.

Worktables or sewing tables became very popular during the late Georgian and Regency period. Typically they had a fabric drawer or pouch for storing the needlework and a lifting hinged top that concealed a set of smaller compartments for sewing items. Card playing amongst men and ladies was popular, so specialist tables with a folding top were produced with rounded corners and dishes to hold either candlesticks or money and counters for gambling. These either had polished top and were used with a cloth or were lined in baize or velvet.

right *During the 18th Century, ladies were encouraged to learn* creative hobbies such as needlework which was particularly *popular with the upper classes, encouraged by the French. Beautiful pieces of furniture were created to house the canvases and wool, and are very collectable today.*

opposite *The drawing room at A La Ronde showing the late 18th-Century room created by the Parminter cousins, who used this room to display their handicrafts, such as shell arrangements and paintings, which were popular pastimes of the day.*

right *Card playing, chess and backgammon were all popular games during the 18th Century, creating a need for beautiful games tables. Many were* demi-lune *or fold-over card tables with intricate inlaid tops opening to form a circular or square table lined with green baize.*

above *This elegant sitting room at Hilltop would have been where Beatrix Potter may have sat and written her famous children stories at the elegant secretaire or, for relaxation, carried out needlework as shown on the stand.*

opposite *Learning an instrument was part of a lady's education and, as entertaining became more popular at home, many upper-class families acquired a piano or a harpsichord. Separate music rooms were a feature of larger homes such as A la Ronde, otherwise the piano would be in the main sitting room.*

"Miss and her sisters sit down by turns, and screw themselves up to "Ah vous dirai", or "I'd be a butterfly" — till some handsome young fellow who has stood behind her chair for six months, turned over her music, or accompanied her through a few liquorish airs, vows his tender passion . . . and at length swears to be her accompaniment through life."

Mirror of Literature, Amusement and Instruction, *a book of original essays*, 1828

B Y Victorian times, living rooms became much more opulent and cluttered, with a greater use of bold colours, patterns and textures. Upholstered furniture was much more comfortable with rounded backs, sprung seats and deep buttoning and adorned with luxurious trimmings. Rococo curved panelling and elaborate plasterwork replaced straight lines and, although panelling was often painted white if not in natural wood, wallpapers by contrast were heavy with strong, bold designs and colour. Technical advances in printing and the manufacture of artificial dyes meant that fabrics were available in just about any material or design you could wish for, from floral chintzes to jacquard weaves to velvets and wools.

Curtains were often surmounted with a stiff, shaped pelmet and trimmed with woven braids or a contrast fabric. The use of fabrics was not just limited to windows and upholstery; the trend for homemade embroidery and needlework led to many ladies making tablecloths, cushions, antimacassars and so on, with the result that every hard surface was either covered by a cloth or by the increasing clutter typical of the period and style. The use of oil and later electric lighting added a welcome feel, and many lamps were draped with beaded shades to diffuse the light.

The layout and use of Victorian living rooms was not dissimilar to earlier in the nineteenth century – they were used for welcoming guests as well as for family activities. Additionally a more masculine room developed – the smoking room – where men could retire and smoke cigars and drink liquors and discuss subjects not deemed suitable for the ladies. In grand houses there was a revival of the idea of the Great Hall, allowing for the Victorian desire to entertain on a large scale, inviting friends, local tenants and labourers alike. Many of these grand spaces were influenced by the designs of A. W. N. Pugin, the English architect best known for his work in the Gothic Revival style, and were fully panelled with large mullioned or stained-glass windows. The use of these halls was not just confined to formal entertaining – they became multifunctional living rooms where games, amateur dramatics and general gatherings took place.

As social visits increased in number, the drawing room now became the room, where ladies would visit one another to take tea or exchange gossip and with other less formal rooms being available for other activities, the drawing room once again became a more formal living room.

The Gothic drawing room at Eastnor Castle was designed by A. W. N. Pugin in 1850. Typical of his style is the lavish plasterwork and colourful ceiling. In spite of the elaborate and grand architecture, comfort is found in the lavish yet relaxed seating which is very much a feature of the Victorian era.

Many early houses had the walls decorated with tapestries rather than paintings, and these, which hang in the North State Drawing Room at Holkham, were said to have been woven by Gerard Peemans at the end of the 17th Century and bought by Lady Leicester in 1759. The tapestries depict the sun's journey through the signs of the zodiac. Many wealthy homeowners commissioned subjects relevant to themselves.

left *The Velvet Room at Ditchley shows exceptional 18th-Century decorative details such as the gilded plasterwork and Genoese silk velvet on the walls which was sent to the 2nd Earl of Litchfield by his brother Admiral Lee in 1738 and still hangs in the room today.*

above *A coloured visual by Alexandre Serebrikoff of the Velvet Room as it was decorated in the mid 20th Century, shows it as a comfortable yet elegant sitting room, similar to the way it would have been at the end of the 18th Century.*

right *Detail of the Genoese silk velvet woven in the Chinoiserie style which was very popular in the 18th Century and used for walls, curtains and upholstery, often using the same designs for everything.*

above *A double-story drawing room with a domed ceiling in a new-build house in Atlanta. The style and detail is of the Adam period, mid to late 18th Century, and the room lends itself to formal entertaining.*

right *The White and Gold Room at Petworth decorated in the French Rococo style, as seen in the decorative plasterwork, the marble chimneypiece and Rococo gilded mirror. Although the house is dated earlier, it was quite typical to have interiors changed by the owners, influenced by the fashion at the time.*

BRINGING an old house to life again and making it work for your own family circumstances while trying to retain its history and character is always a challenge, and yet more of a challenge if the building is listed and requires planning approval. A qualified architect will know the procedure and will hopefully be aware of what changes will be acceptable and what will not.

The main part of this particular house dates from 1719 and the bulk of it was remodelled in 1881. It was originally built to the typically Jacobean H-shaped plan and is now more of a U-shape, but at one point in the nineteenth century, the now rear courtyard had been built over to create a Great Hall, which although a wonderful space for entertaining, took natural light and views away from the original entrance hall. Fortunately this was removed in the mid twentieth century. Our task was to make the different areas and styles work as one. This involved changing a very

insignificant concealed staircase into a substantial secondary staircase serving the more utilitarian wing of the house and providing decent access to guest bedrooms, and changing the use of a series of utility rooms. This resulted in several rooms becoming more important than they had been, so they, too, had to be remodelled. The garden room had a series of windows of differing sizes, which looked wrong internally and externally, so these were changed to match existing stone mullions. The opposite wing, which is Georgian in style, has sash windows as opposed to stone mullions and some original panelling. The drawing room had a strange Jacobean-style strapwork ceiling which had been added later, and I was very keen to remove it, as it ruined the proportions of the room. Fortunately, after quite a struggle and a lot of research, we were able to prove it was not the real thing, and the planners allowed us to reinstate a Georgian cornice and restore the room to its original feel.

An old black-and-white photograph showing the drawing room of this Jacobean house before recent restoration. The heavy strapwork ceiling and panelling were typical of the details of that time and made the room feel heavy and oppressive.

An old black-and-white photograph of the main staircase which shows the dark panelling in a wood finish typical of the Jacobean or Victorian period.

top right *By removing the heavy strapwork ceiling and adding a new sash window, this previously heavy room has been transformed into a bright, sunny and well-proportioned room.*

right *The newly-decorated main staircase. The old panelling has been painted in two tones of decorative paint finish which makes it feel lighter. The balusters and columns were originally wood then they were painted and now they are back to their natural oak finish.*

This beautiful pine-panelled room had been used as a film location and damaged so it needed to be restored to its former glory with careful repairs and a wax finish to the wood-work. The ceiling panels are not original to the room; the present owners bought them as four corner sections, so once installed they required additional work and restoration to make them look like one continuous piece. The cloud ceiling was also added and the result is an elegant 18th-Century sitting room.

"I find out what the world needs. Then, I go ahead and invent it."

Thomas Alva Edison (1847–1931)
Inventor of the electric light bulb

right *Two views of an elegant Georgian-style drawing room that was a recent addition to a Cotswold farmhouse. It was built with features in keeping with the rest of the house, such as the stone mullion windows and leaded lights, which are double-glazed. The advantage of building from scratch is that you can achieve the right proportions and add details such as the built-in bookcase. The oak plank floor is typical of the period and leads off the large barn beyond.*

HAPPY THOUGHT.

The Electric Light, so favourable to Furniture, Wall Papers, Pictures, Screens, &c., is not always becoming to the Female Complexion. Light Japanese Sunshades will be found invaluable.

ELECTRICITY CHANGES EVERYTHING

The early Victorian home was lit by smoky oil lamps and candles housed in chandeliers, wall sconces and candelabra. Gas, although used for street lighting early in the century, was distrusted in the home until the 1850s, when gas fittings were introduced into the Houses of Parliament. In 1880, a mansion in Newcastle built in the Arts and Crafts style by Norman Shaw was the first home in Britain to install clean and convenient electric lighting. It took a while to catch on though, and early fittings, which made great play of showing off the newfangled incandescent light bulb, were not the easiest of lights to manage. Most homes towards the end of the 19th Century used gas lamps, candles and electric lighting, and it wasn't until after the First World War that electricity became the norm.

The double parlour at Millford Hall, *a fine Greek Revival plantation house in South Carolina. The areas are split with large, imposing Corinthian columns and the folding doors have inset mirrored panels which, along with the mirrors over the fireplaces, help give additional light and depth to the room. It is a very formal room with good proportions and perfectly designed for giving parties.*

TODAY the use of living rooms on a day to day basis is generally far less formal, and depending on the size of the house and how many other rooms are available, a modern living space may double up as family room and place for entertaining. Most homes will have, in addition to a living room, a large informal family room. This is often an extension to, or part of, the kitchen and breakfast room, where the TV and computers etc are placed. If there are young children, this room is often turned into a playroom where children can create their own havoc and get creative with their toys. In any event, if space permits, it is nice to have one room that can be kept more formal and less cluttered, where you can escape for peace and quiet to read or entertain guests without having to clear away toys or stow papers.

Many new build American houses have an open plan layout with rooms on the ground floor (first floor in the United States) leading from one to another without doors impeding the flow. This would tend to lead to a less formal look, however this is not necessarily the case, as many American houses are a lot larger than a equivalent family home in Europe, and there are more rooms for different purposes. There is often a large kitchen with an adjacent family or breakfast room, a library, a formal sitting room, a separate dining room and a den or media room.

Where the open-plan idea comes into its own is in the urban loft apartment carved into huge former industrial buildings, or barn conversions in country areas. In these magnificent, high-ceilinged spaces, many owners have chosen to go back to the Great Hall concept with few internal walls to interrupt the architecture.

above *A recently-restored barn which was pretty much derelict and not attached to the main house. It is now a multifunction entertaining room*

opposite *A recently-restored first-floor family room in a Tudor wing of a large country house. The room has original features and new additions in the form of a mezzanine floor accessed by a contemporary staircase.*

previous page *View of the restored barn shown on page 107 from the fireplace end, looking at one of the upper galleries formed from large reclaimed oak beams and new oak panelling in Jacobean style. The stonework was meticulously restored and sockets floor-mounted in order to preserve the stonework.*

right *A pine-panelled drawing room in a newly built house in Dallas. The panelling is in the Georgian style with a continental twist in the curved top panels and windows. The lit cabinet was specifically designed to house china and glass collections, and lights were strategically placed to highlight artwork.*

above *The work of Frank Lloyd Wright has to be judged from the inside out and the outside in. This is the exterior of the house he designed for himself and his lover Mamah Cheyney in the Wisconsin River valley, where he had spent his summer holidays as a child. These photographs were taken during the architect's lifetime.*

right *The living room at Taliesin with the huge chimney wall that rises through the roof. Frank Lloyd Wright excelled in creating open-plan living spaces that flowed effortlessly into one another, creating shapes and spaces within spaces. He used combinations of natural materials, stone, plaster and wood to define and emphasize proportions.*

"'Think simple' as my old master
used to say – meaning reduce the
whole of its parts into the simplest
terms, getting back to
first principles."

Frank Lloyd Wright (1867–1959)
American architect

This loft apartment in New York City shows how open-plan living can be very effective if the space is well planned. Clever use of materials such as glass walls help divide areas without making them claustrophobic, and although privacy and storage can be an issue, the overall look is very appealing.

above *The drawing room of this new Dallas home, although a defined living space, is very much part of the stair hall and general open-plan layout of the ground floor. Doors can take up a lot of wall space and prevent light from filtering through to other spaces and, in this case, the room feels a lot larger than it is by virtue of having no doors. With open-plan living it is important for colours to flow from one area to another.*

right *A contemporary New York City loft furnished with design classics and flooded with natural light from a wall of arched windows. Space is cleverly subdivided with three-quarter-height walls and glass panels above.*

"Design is a plan for arranging
elements in such a way as best to
accomplish a particular purpose."

Charles Eames (1847–1931)
American designer

Library

18 + 0
27

Office

19 + 0
27

Passage

Study

14 + 6
27

12 + 6
17

Den

10 + 6
8

51. 0

44 6

LIBRARIES

A LIBRARY as a separate room did not exist until the late seventeenth and early eighteenth centuries, when it evolved as a room to display and store all the Classical artifacts acquired during a gentleman's Grand Tour of Europe and his growing collection of books. The library was traditionally a masculine space decorated with panelling, which sometimes incorporated bookcases displaying a combination of books, busts and works of art. Some earlier houses that were remodelled in the eighteenth century used the now-redundant long gallery as a library with the addition of shelving or bookcases.

By the beginning of the nineteenth century, and with the desire for a less formal style of living, the library became more of a general sitting room, where the family would take tea, play cards, sew, etc. It was often situated adjacent to another living room so the two rooms could be joined together with double or, in rare cases, sliding doors.

By Victorian times, the library had reverted back to a male domain, a room where the owner would meet and entertain his male guests, sit and drink before and after meals and smoke cigars. Many libraries constructed during the Victorian period were in the Gothic style, such as at Strawberry Hill or Eaton Hall, with ornate and somewhat romantic and Ecclesiastical-style arches and arched top bookcases and fireplaces.

THE shape and architecture of this room has changed little since it was built by Nicholas Hawksmoor in 1694 and decorated for the owner, the Earl of Pomfret, in the 1830s. The large, imposing bookcases were, however, designed and added by the legendary David Hicks in the 1970s for the previous owner and whilst immensely practical, they do overshadow and detract from the original proportions and architectural details. Personally, I find the heavy projecting cornice and large square columns too dominant and the best way to make them blend into the room was to paint the walls and panelling and bookcases in the same tones, in this case subtle beiges and off-whites.

The overall effect we were after was to make the room look like a gentleman's retreat, with a display of books and objects that could have been collected on the Grand Tour of Europe in the eighteenth century. Imposing bookcases such as these look infinitely better with beautiful leather-bound books and, to break the linear feel, the interjection of a piece of sculpture, a small painting on a stand or a beautiful artifact. The busts on top of the columns work well in this room and help anchor the large projecting cornice.

"A library is a delivery room for the birth of ideas, a place where history comes to life."

Norman Cousins (1915–1990)
American political journalist and peace activist

previous page and right *The bookshelves in this library, which were designed by David Hicks, were installed by the previous owner. The present owner has filled them with an orderly collection of leather-bound books and spaced the shelves to fit the books. The library is a light and bright, masculine room. The rug is an Aubusson and furniture is in the French style.*

left *This elegant Jacobean-style oak library was recently installed into a Tudor wing of an old house and gives the impression of having always been there. The cleverly-designed jib door disguises a staircase that leads to another area.*

above *A view of the opposite wall showing detail of the bay window reveal and the second concealed jib door in the closed position.*

above right *View of the same concealed jib door, now open, revealing access to a stone spiral staircase which leads up and down to various rooms.*

right *Detail showing the linenfold panelling and carved detail on the main door to the library.*

above *The Library at Biltmore House in North Carolina built for George Washington Vanderbilt II. The two-story-height room contains over 10,000 books specially bound in rich, gilded leather.*

right *A Victorian-style library at Sandon Hall, a Neo-Jacobean house in Staffordshire built by William Burn for the 2nd Earl of Harrowby, who was a serious academic as his library bears witness.*

BOOKPLATES

When books were leather bound, gilt blocked, rare and precious items, they were available only to the rich who could afford them. As these valuable repositories of knowledge were accumulated into libraries, owners began to identify their books first by a gilded stamp on the cover or a simple inscription and then by pasting in specially printed bookplates, usually bearing the words *ex libris* (meaning from the books of) followed by an heraldic device and the name of the owner. As time went by, more attention was lavished on the design of the bookplate, to reflect not only the fashion in decorative art of the time but also the taste and sensibilities of the owner.

left *The Library at Batemans, the Jacobean home where Rudyard Kipling lived. The bookshelves are simple in style and more Arts and Crafts in feel but ideal for his display of books and artifacts collected on his travels.*

right *The main part of the Library at Muncaster Castle was built in 1780, on the site of the old medieval kitchens, for the first Baron Muncaster who started the collection of books. Some of the bookcases were added in 1862, so the room has more of a Victorian feel.*

SPECIALIST library furniture was soon in demand, for instance library tables with polished or marble tops and decorative carving on the frieze and legs, knee-hole desks and writing tables. Early Queen Anne–style bookcases were replaced with large break-fronted mahogany bookcases with a broken pediment, pilasters and decorative cornice. Some bookcases were left open whilst others had glass doors with fine glazing bars in a variety of shapes. Display cabinets with a glazed upper part and perhaps a drawer below were also popular and specifically designed to display china or curios, such as coins and stones collected on the Grand Tour. During the Rococo period it became fashionable for some of these pieces to have a lacquer or Chinoiserie finish and later many were inlaid with brass and other materials such as mother-of-pearl.

By the Regency period, many styles of chairs were available, either fully upholstered or with cane seat and sides with a loose seat cushion. Library chairs which turned into steps were a novel but useful piece. Dwarf bookcases, a low piece with either open shelves or doors with a brass grill and fabric behind, were also popular.

The Victorian study was typically cluttered with worktables and games tables with wood inlays and papier-mâché with inlaid brasswork and mother-of-pearl. And there were plenty of other smaller pieces to trip over, such as firescreens with embroidered panels, buttoned footstools, canterburies for holding papers and magazines and carved pedestal plant stands – basically the more the merrier.

This study in a Chelsea terraced house was used by Thomas Carlyle from 1834 to 1881. The attic was a peaceful working atmosphere away from street noise.

left *The Mount, a Classical Revival house based on the English principles of the H style, was built in 1902 by the celebrated author Edith Wharton. The design of the Library follows the recommendations in* The Design of Houses *that the prime purpose of a library should be for the display of books, with bookcases built into the walls rather than freestanding. This image shows how the room looked after I decorated it for a design showcase event and depicts how it may have looked had Edith Wharton built it today. The furniture was specially commissioned by myself and made by David Linley.*

TODAY It is rare to have a separate library especially in town houses with space at a premium. But with working from home so much more prevalent, most homes now have a home office or study that tends to be lined with bookcases. It is now considered quite normal to house books in any room, from the sitting room or kitchen to the bedroom, and in fact the addition of books is often a visual plus. Books do, after all, furnish a room, and to have them all confined to one place, unless of course it happens to be an existing library in a large Classical period house, feels wrong.

Where we have lost the library, we have gained the media room, thus removing from the living room all the technology of modern communications and the ubiquitous TV, a great compromise especially for period homes, where large screens look so out of place and much ingenuity goes into hiding wiring and cabling. And coming full circle, as most things do, the gentleman's retreat has become the den: a comfortable, relaxed, laid-back space where male members of the household retreat to watch sport, drink and discuss topics of little or no interest to the ladies.

far left *The study at Batemans, Rudyard Kipling's home, with the original Jacobean oak beams and stone mullioned windows – the bookcases were built in later. The French walnut draw-leaf table provides a good alternative work surface to a desk and shows all his writing tools.*

left *How to give period-style homes all the technology they need? Hide the hub in an elegant cupboard.*

Many old studies or traditional libraries have become family sitting rooms with large TV screens dominating the room. In this new-build house in Dallas, the purpose-built den/TV room is in the basement, where the vaulted ceiling and brick walls give the room character. It is divided into separate areas for seating, eating and TV watching.

"I find television very educating. Every time somebody turns on the set, I go into the other room and read a book."

Groucho Marx (1890–1977)
American comedian, film star and wit

A contemporary den that has been specifically designed for TV viewing, with large, comfortable seating and the screen built flush into the wall. Serious movie-watchers can enjoy comfortable seating and a large size screen.

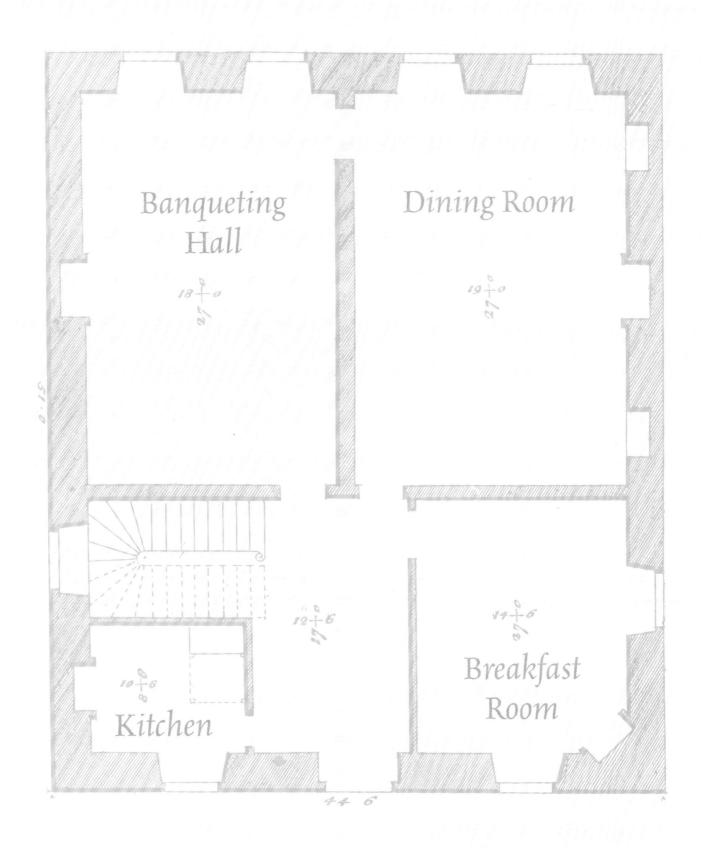

DINING ROOMS

THE art of dining has always been about offering hospitality, entertainment and sustenance to family, friends and neighbours, whether the venue is a cavernous Great Hall with the lord of the manor at the head of his trestle table or a cosy, intimate twenty-first-century kitchen supper.

The sixteenth-century dining room was sparsely decorated and located conveniently next to the kitchen, with panelling and tapestries or fabric hangings later replaced by pictures, as they did not retain food smells. A gate-leg table typically sat against the wall with chairs pulled out for use. A court cupboard, or an alcove built in with shelves, housed drinking vessels and dishes and the room was lit with candlelight.

By the early eighteenth century, with entertaining becoming fashionable, the formal dining room evolved. One of the first such examples was the Marble Parlour designed by William Kent at Houghton, designed to impress with plasterwork by John Michael Rysbrak, representing Bacchus, a typical theme for many eighteenth-century dining rooms. As house design developed, the size and importance of the dining room equalled that of the drawing room. Servants' living quarters and kitchens were now kept well away from family areas (sometimes in separate pavilions) to protect from fire, noise and smells. The butler's pantry, a staging post between kitchen and dining room, from which meals could be served, was a necessary innovation and accessed by a hidden door or "jib door" cleverly designed into the panelling to allow servants to come and go discreetly.

The eighteenth-century dining room was generally panelled with larger panels above the dado rail, either hung with leather or damask or left plain to take pictures, and below plain wall or small panels. By the Rococo period walls were adorned with elaborate plasterwork and panelling and sometimes fabric. Robert Adam designed many elaborate dining rooms, such as those at Kedleston and Saltram, with ornate Neo-Classical panelling, plasterwork ceilings, specific alcoves and niches to display works of art and sculptures and carpets that reflected the design of the ceiling.

Dining rooms were evening rooms. Breakfast was an informal meal served anytime between 9:00 a.m. and noon, often served for men in the breakfast room or parlour and for women in their bedrooms set up on small mahogany breakfast tables. The main meal of the day was dinner and could be anytime from noon to 5:00 p.m., but as it became fashionable to eat later, the gap between breakfast and dinner was filled with lunch – initially a snack referred to as "nunchin" or something eaten between meals.

The dining room at Easton Neston was originally the drawing room leading off the Great Hall; however in the late 19th Century, a passage was created to lead to what is now the dining room. The plasterwork is said to be by local stuccoist John Woolston. The central ceiling medallion depicts Venus and Adonis. The Palladian-style fireplace is in Carrara marble, and the two chandeliers are copies of the original.

The North Dining Room at Holkham Hall, the Palladian house built by the Earl of Burlington and William Kent between 1736 and 1764. The apse at one end conceals small doors giving access for the servants to reach the kitchen.

The dining room at Marble House built for William K. Vanderbilt by Richard Morris Hunt between 1888 and 1892. The walls are marble with gilded details – inspiration was from Le Petit Trianon at Versailles.

THE 200-YARD DASH

In some grand houses, the distance from kitchen to dining room could be as far as 220 yards, and it wasn't a straight run. Footmen, whose job it was to deliver hot food from kitchen to dining room, had to be nimble and strong as well as fast on their feet as they negotiated narrow staircases, heavy doors and twisting passages. These natural athletes were also in demand for competitive walking races that attracted handsome fees, heavy wagers and eventually international recognition. The present-day tradition of racewalking can be traced back directly to the footman and his silver salver fleet-footing around the stately homes of Great Britain.

above *A Victorian-style dining room at Tyntesfield in Somerset which shows Gothic features typical of the time in the panelled ceiling and carved details of the fire surround. Note the hidden cupboard by the fireplace, possibly used to hide spices or alcohol.*

right *The dining room of a newly-built house in Dallas with custom-designed niches/storage cabinets to house the antique stained-glass panels. The fire surround was also custom-made.*

opposite above The dining room at A la Ronde leads off the Octagon Hall and is a good example of a small Regency room, cleverly designed with a niche to take a sideboard or serving table.

opposite below This dining room at Kingscote, a Gothic Revival house in Newport, Rhode Island, was remodelled by McKim, Mead and White in the 1870s. It shows an interesting combination of Colonial American and Arts and Crafts details and the use of new materials such as cork tiles, seen on the walls and ceiling, and opalescent glass bricks by Louis Comfort Tiffany.

below The dining room at the Winslow Crocker House at Cape Cod. The 18th-Century house was moved from a previous location and remodelled to house Mary Thacher's collection of early 20th-Century American furniture and artifacts.

D INING furniture developed along with the customs of the time. When dinner could last for five hours, dining furniture needed to be comfortable and practical as well as formal. Until large mahogany dining tables with leaves became fashionable, separate smaller tables would be brought in and used with chairs placed around the perimeter of the room. A huge number of new pieces were made: sideboards with plate warmers and cellarets for wine, urns to store knives and cold drinks, serving tables with plate racks and cutlery drawers, china cabinets and dumb waiters. Chairs were upholstered with horsehair and leather rather than fabric, which retained the smell of food.

At this time, food was laid out on the main table and guests helped themselves or had to rely on a servant or neighbour to ensure they were passed the dish they desired. During the nineteenth century, it was more fashionable to serve *à la Russe* whereby the table was laid with a place setting and food was served to each guest by a bevy of footmen.

Victorian dining did not disappoint; it was paramount to their well-being to be well fed and essential to their social standing to entertain suitably. Breakfast for the wealthy, who now went out to work, was a substantial meal to ensure they were fortified for what lay ahead and, in some more formal houses, was preceded by formal prayers for the entire household. Entertaining at lunchtime was a feminine pursuit, a meal generally eaten in the dining room. Dinner was still the most important meal and served around 7:00 or 8:00 p.m. The art of giving a good dinner party became an essential part of a family's social standing. Etiquette was paramount, from the sending of invitations to the dress worn to the food and wine served and, of course, the decoration of the table.

"... the dining room was dark, and possessed none of those appearances of plenteous hospitality which dining rooms should have."

Anthony Trollope (1815–1882) English novelist in *Can You Forgive Her?*, 1856

above and left *The dining room at Chartwell, the home of Sir Winston Churchill, showing a relaxed informal setting with comfortable chairs and rush matting. It was used by Churchill for meetings and to screen films. The image below shows his own painting of the room with himself and guests in 1928.*

right *This dining/living room is in a renovated barn. The fireplace and gallery were added to provide a wonderful large entertaining space. The custom-made table can seat 20 people.*

SEPARATE formal dining rooms continued to be part of everyday life up until the First World War, when the need for an army of servants and the chance to entertain on a grand scale decreased. Although many country houses continued to use the dining room for special occasions, daily use was made of breakfast rooms adjacent to the kitchen or entirely new family kitchens, where the lady of the house learned to take on the role of cook. This pattern has pretty much continued today with the kitchen/breakfast room becoming the hub of the house, incorporating an informal eating area and a seating area to watch TV or read a newspaper.

The formal dining room is, in many cases, redundant but rather than leave it empty, it can be put to more practical use perhaps doubling as a home office or study and an occasional entertaining space. It is not necessary to have a permanent dining table, as it is easy enough to set one up as needed and cover it with an attractive cloth. A long table with an indestructible surface can have two identities – for working or dining – and round tables can have a larger top made for them that can be stored in two halves and deployed when required. Additional chairs can be stored or used in other areas of the house, and I like the idea of using a mixture of chair styles around the table.

This large single kitchen/dining room has the space conveniently divided into distinct working and eating areas by the breakfast bar which also provides a space to perch and have a cup of coffee. The wood beams add character and an interesting architectural feature to the room.

above *The breakfast area at one end of the kitchen of a new house in Dallas has lovely views over the garden.*

left *This new Shaker-style kitchen is fresh and bright with a lovely limestone floor. The wood beams and table add warmth to the space.*

right *The eating and seating area of a country house kitchen make for a multifunctional room.*

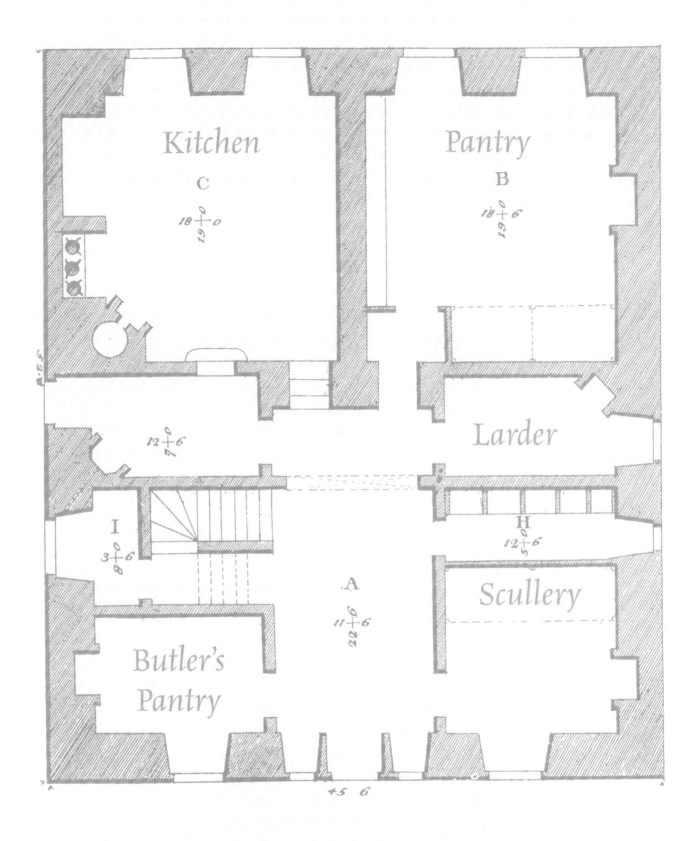

KITCHENS

Early kitchens were basic, and only once plumbing had been installed were sinks fitted to the wall. One of the sinks at Lanhydrock in Cornwall is slate lined for preparing vegetables, the other zinc lined for washing up. Simple wood racks were used for drying and storing plates. The copper pan collection on the previous page is at Holkham Hall.

EARLY medieval kitchens were built off the main hall behind a screen and at the opposite end of the Great Hall from the raised dais where the family ate. A large kitchen complex including buttery, pantry and storage cellars was needed to cater for large communal meals – family, household staff, land workers – maybe 100 to 300 people per day.

As the risk of fire was so great, the main kitchen was often built in a separate pavilion reached by a passageway. Meat was cooked on an open fire on a spit and pots were placed on an arm hanging over the fire – bread was made in a separate area in a brick-lined oven. Many houses ended up with one kitchen serving the staff and another built nearer to the family's living quarters. Cooking and menial tasks were carried out by men, whilst the ladies made jams and preserved fruit. There was much to be done: water had to be collected from wells and the fire was kept burning continually, the ashes covered overnight by a "curfew" from the French *couvre-feu* (cover fire), and restarted the next morning.

By the seventeenth century, the plan of the house changed dramatically but the kitchen was still kept well out of the way, as architects of grand houses had no intention of letting smoke, smells and noise ruin their glory. Kitchens were consigned to the basement with stone-vaulted ceilings to provide insulation from noise and fire, and whitewashed walls and flagstone floors. They had built-in chimneys for ventilation, and sash windows, placed high up in the walls, allowed for privacy and ensured staff were not distracted from their work. Coal replaced wood as the main fuel and the open hearth was gradually replaced by a cast-iron hob grate, which subsequently developed into the range cooker. This arrangement continued pretty much until Victorian times, when household habits and standards of living changed.

"...There are only three things I need to make my kitchen a pleasant one so long as it is clean. First I need space enough to get a good simple meal for six people ... Then I need a window or two, for clear air and a sight of things growing ... Most of all I need to be alone. I need peace."

From *The Art of Eating* by M. F. K. Fisher (1908–1992) American food writer

HIERARCHY BELOW STAIRS

Status and respect for position was just as important among servants as it was in the rest of 18th- and 19th-Century society. Upper servants and senior servants expected deference from underservants, and underservants aspired to rise through the ranks. At the top of the female servant ladder were the housekeeper and the lady's maid. On the next rung were the senior servants – the governess and nurse. Top underservant was the cook followed by the head housemaid and head kitchen maid, followed by the rest of the kitchen and household staff. Last in the pecking order was the scullery maid. Top male servants were the butler and the valet, who did for his master what the lady's maid did for his wife. The coachman and head gardener enjoyed senior servant status. Underservants included footmen, grooms and the rest of the gardening staff.

This sophisticated two-tier butler's pantry is at the Breakers, the lavish mansion built for Cornelius Vanderbilt. When entertaining on a grand scale it was essential to have the right items to dress the table and serve food. Silver and china would have followed the family from mansion to mansion.

FROM early medieval times, there were separate rooms for different functions, and this custom has continued in larger houses until this day. The pantry, traditionally placed nearer to the eating quarters than the kitchen, was used for preparation and storage of dry goods whilst the scullery was for preparation of meats, game and fish and cleaning up. The larder, from the French *lard*, (salted bacon) was used for storage of preserved meats and luxury items. Salt was a precious commodity – often stored in secret locations such as a hole in the wall. Larger households had several larders, for wet and dry foods and for meat and pastry. The buttery, or butlery, was where wine, beer and ale was served from, so it was often located nearest to the Great Hall.

In smaller houses, the buttery and pantry doubled up as one room so everything that didn't require cooking was stored and served from there, including tableware. If the kitchen was located a long way from the dining room, then food was assembled and kept warm in a servery. Many large houses also had a still-room, originally used by the lady of the house to prepare medicines, beer and wine, cleaning products, etc., from home-grown produce. It then became the domain of the housekeeper, where jams, pickles and cakes were made and later where light meals such as afternoon tea or picnics were prepared.

this page *The dairy scullery at Lanhydrock, which was used specifically for making butter, cream and cheese from milk produced on the estate. Different areas of the kitchen were split up into separate preparation areas. Many kitchen and sculleries were in the basements of large houses and designed with large, high windows to allow for good ventilation.*

opposite above *Stone walls helped to keep basement kitchens cool, as shown here in the scullery at Castle Drogo.*

opposite *The butler's pantry at Cragside, Northumberland, including the workbenches and butler's equipment. This small room has easy access to the front door, kitchen, dining room and reception rooms.*

left *Large houses had separate storage rooms or larders for different foods to ensure good hygiene and no cross-contamination. Special meat and poultry rooms such as this one at Saltram had meat hooks to hang game and joints of meat. The Victorian wall tiles helped keep the room cool.*

right *The china room at Blenheim, with its beautiful stone-vaulted ceiling, leads onto the Italian gardens. It was originally part of the servants' area but is now used for occasional informal meals and houses random pieces of family china.*

THE early eighteenth century saw a new emerging middle class and households slimmed down from around 100 personnel to 20. Household staff were predominantly confined to the basement for work and meals, and to the attics for sleeping – it was not considered appropriate for them to be seen.

In Victorian times a tax was imposed on male servants in a drive to get them to join the forces, so most domestic staff were now female with the exception of the butler and possibly chef – it was very fashionable to have a French chef or one with a knowledge of French cuisine. With the introduction of labour-saving devices such as gas lighting, gas geysers, running water and built-in ovens, the task of running a household and producing meals became easier and less labour intensive. Mrs. Beeton was truly inspirational at this time – the Martha Stewart or Delia Smith of the time – and her *Book of Household Management* transformed the Victorian household below and above stairs advising on all aspects of "modern" life. She advocated glazed tiles on the kitchen walls with a blue tint to discourage flies and cement or a smooth surface on the floor for ease of cleaning.

top right *A Victorian-style kitchen in a Welsh house dating back to the 15th Century. The beams are original and the dresser-style units, with old-fashioned plate racks in between, were made in keeping with the age of the property.*

right *A very basic 1950s-style kitchen at Mendips, where John Lennon lived and where his aunt Mimi would cook him his favourite meal of fish and chips washed down with a cup of tea.*

opposite *The kitchen/scullery at Wrightwick Manor is typical of Victorian kitchens with range cooker and large work table.*

THE development of modern kitchens into sociable spaces in which to develop home cooking as a pleasurable and creative art form can be attributed to pioneers such as Julia Child in America and Elizabeth David in England. They both had a love of French cuisine and Mediterranean·ingredients, and both researched and wrote about their passion. Travelling extensively in Europe and savouring delicious fresh ingredients and observing the love and knowledge that French and Italian home cooks bought to the table, they lit a flame in their respective countries at a time when wartime restrictions were ending and there was a huge appetite for change.

COOKBOOKS

Instructions for the preparation of food have been around since the 2nd Century BC, and tens of thousands of tomes published since taking the didactic domestic science route for the erudition of household staff and the good plain cook. It took someone in love with the sensual delights of food and cooking to change all that, and for us Brits that person was the glamorous and dashing Elizabeth David, who woke up the jaded postwar ration palate with a beautifully expressed enthusiasm for olive oil, ripe tomatoes and Mediterranean country food.

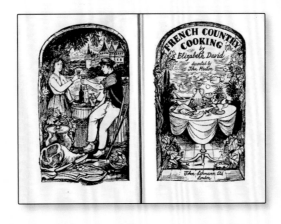

"How can a nation be called great
if its bread tastes like Kleenex?"

Julia Child

IN most houses today, certainly those without any household staff, the kitchen is the hub of the house and the most important room in terms of renovation, expenditure and investment. The cost of a new kitchen can be quite a shock – but it doesn't need to be. Many kitchens have so many bells and whistles and gimmicks, most of which the average cook or family will never appreciate or use.

Kitchens are very personal and habit forming, so it's important to have input from the end user when designing a layout. Choice of style is endless and in my view comes down to the style of the house, what you like and what will work for your lifestyle.

These are the key issues to consider: The layout needs to be split into preparation, cooking, storage, washing up and eating areas. Functional appliances must be considered and appropriate lighting and ventilation. Floor, wall and cabinet finishes should be chosen not only for appearance but, taking a leaf from Mrs. Beeton's *Book of Houshold Management*, for ease of cleaning.

The shape of the room and space available will determine the basic layout. Start with placing essential items and appliances and then build the working areas and storage around them. If space is available, I would learn lessons from the past and install a separate larder and storage area.

A painted contemporary kitchen manufactured by Smallbone in a new-build house in Dallas. The owner is an avid cook so each area and the layout were carefully designed to work for her specific needs. The floor is Amtico and the worktops are a combination of wood, tile and marble.

above *A new industrial-style kitchen built in the newly renovated basement at Easton Neston. It is laid out like a Victorian kitchen but has all the advantages of modern equipment. The character is retained with the stone floor and walls and coffered ceilings.*

opposite *When a kitchen is part of an open-plan eating and living area, it makes sense for the kitchen to blend with the room. The two examples here make use of custom-made wooden cabinetry and discreet appliances.*

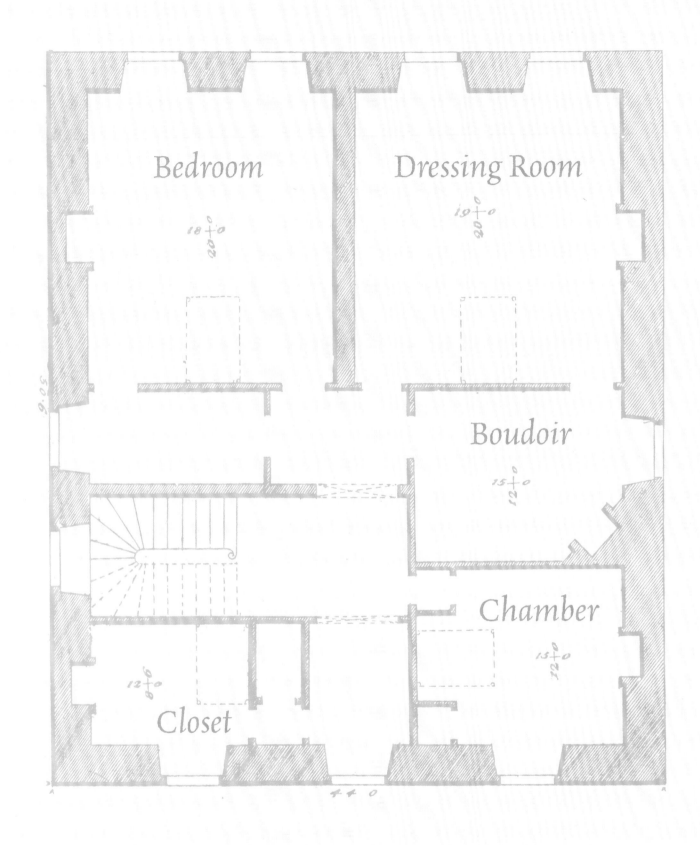

BEDROOMS

THE bedroom or bedchamber as a separate room did not develop until the mid-eighteenth century; until then there was communal sleeping in the Great Hall and perhaps a separate Great Chamber complex off the hall where the family ate, sat and slept or received important guests. Great Chambers were only found in grander houses, sometimes with a separate bedchamber for sleeping and a withdrawing chamber where the servant would bed down for the night whilst his master slept.

During the seventeenth century, the importance of the Great Chamber grew but it was still a multifunctional room, a grand bed-sitting room with the bed the most prominent piece of furniture, sometimes placed on a raised platform with a rail in front of it or in an alcove so that curtains could be drawn in front of it. The withdrawing chamber became a more generally accessible space where people would meet and wait before being invited into the Great Chamber. In addition, there would be a closet where only the most important people would be invited to discuss social or business affairs.

State bedrooms at this time were sumptuously decorated with fabric or specially commissioned tapestries on the wall. Whilst in the fifteenth and sixteenth centuries, the bed was heavily carved with large posts and headboard with a canopy over it, the fabric hangings were relatively simple, often in a heavy-weight fabric, trimmed with braid or fringe, the main purpose of which was keeping out the draughts.

Many grand houses had state bedrooms lavishly decorated to accommodate visiting dignitaries or guests for weekend house parties. The four-poster bed was always the focal point and a status symbol. The parrot bedroom at Holkham Hall has a bed with a carved gilded pelmet and elaborate bed dressings in the same fabric as the walls.

"In bed we laugh, in bed we cry;
And born in bed, in bed we die;
The near approach a bed may show
Of human bliss to human woe."

Isaac de Benserade (1613–1691) French poet

By the seventeenth century, the bed was extremely ornate and an important status symbol with elaborate carved posts and either a carved or fabric-covered cornice and padded fabric headboard all covered in the same fabric. The window draperies and upholstery would have been in the same fabric as the bed curtains, an influence taken from France, and the use of passementerie – elaborate fringing, bobbles and tassels – increased along with availability.

below *George Vanderbilt's bedroom at Biltmore House in North Carolina, which was completed in 1895. The room has a masculine feel with bold crimson fabrics and heavy, carved furniture. He was an avid reader and collector and was able to access his library gallery (see page 124) from a secret door leading from this room.*

opposite *The bedroom of my great-grandmother, Consuelo Vanderbilt, at her parents' home in Marble House in Newport, Rhode Island. She was a very feminine, elegant lady, and I find it interesting that she would have such a heavy, masculine bedroom which is more representative of a Tudor room than a grand Gilded Age mansion whose interiors tend to French Rococo influence.*

As the layout of the house began to change at the end of the seventeenth century and beginning of the eighteenth century, with servants quarters moved to the basement and the introduction of back stairs, so the grand bedchamber moved from ground level to the first floor – although it remained on the main level in existing grand houses. The new layout allowed for a single apartment consisting of a bedroom, dressing room and closet, and in many households the husband and wife had separate yet adjoining suites. The bedroom was no longer a public space and was typically smaller than the dressing room which acted more like a sitting room where the lady would spend most of her morning and close family could be received or where meals could be taken. The gentleman of the house often had two dressing rooms, one off the bedroom and one on the main floor where he could conduct business whilst he continued with his toilet and dressing for the day.

In addition, the lady may have had a boudoir which was used earlier on as a washing and dressing area and in Victorian times as an evening sitting room or a romantic place to entertain a male companion.

At this time, beds were still important and often four posters, but additional bedroom furniture appeared: free-standing wardrobes or linen presses, dressing tables, chests of drawers, night washstands with a china bowl for washing and commodes incorporating a chamber pot.

this page *A guest bedroom decorated in a French style with* toile de jouy *on the four-poster bed and curtains: typical of late 18th-Century bedrooms.*

opposite *A Regency-style bedroom decorated by my company at Easton Neston. The green two-tone stripe fabric was specially commissioned – the furniture is antique.*

opposite *A principal guest bedroom at Easton Neston. The four-poster bed was inherited from the previous owners and has an interesting painted cornice.*

above left *The unusual corner fireplace provides a useful display area, and gilded brackets add a decorative feature. The panelling is original and painted in subtle tones of creams*

above right *An 18th-Century tapestry helps add authenticity to the Baroque architecture. Note the printed toile fabric and bullion fringe on the bed pelmet.*

BY the end of the eighteenth century, more fabrics were being imported and produced in England and were therefore more affordable, so bed hangings became varied and lighter. Printed cottons and embroidered silks with naturalistic designs replaced heavy velvets, tapestries and wool damasks and, as before, were used for both windows and beds. French Rococo decoration was a main influence, as was the publication in 1754 of books such as Thomas Chippendale's *The Gentleman and Cabinet Makers Director*. The trend was towards Rococo bedrooms with Polonaise beds and Chinoiserie-style bedrooms with hand-painted wallpaper and Chinese-inspired silks, furnished with Chinese Chippendale carved beds and chairs. By the Regency period, bedrooms and bed treatments became even lighter and airier and heavily draped pelmets were considered unhealthy, as they accumulated dusts and smells. Four-poster beds were replaced by half testers with stiff, shaped pelmets, and metal bed frames were covered with light chintzes or sheers. In the nineteenth century, the layout of the upstairs family quarters still consisted of main bedroom, dressing room for the man and boudoir for the lady. Children's bedrooms and nurseries were typically on the floor above. In larger houses, a whole wing was allocated for the family's quarters over two floors, with guest bedrooms in an adjacent wing. The best rooms were reserved for married couples and single ladies; bachelors were often confined to a separate corridor or floor.

left *A beautiful custom-made Gothic-style bed, commissioned by my clients for a guest bedroom in the Tudor wing of their house. The marquetry panels depict a love story.*

above right *Detail of the hand-carved Gothic-style pelmet and the shaped fabric pelmets framing the bay window.*

STORING CLOTHES

In medieval times, clothes were stored in chests that were often the only other pieces of furniture in a house apart from the bed and the board (trestle table). As clothing for the rich became more elaborate and costly, special rooms were set aside for the storage of apparel. The rooms, called garderobes, basically a private chamber attached to the bedroom, often housed an open-drop lavatory built into the thickness of the walls. The actual piece of furniture clothes that were kept in was called a press and divided into a hanging section and shelves to lay clothes out flat. Eventually the garderobe became a piece of furniture called a wardrobe, which sufficed most families until recently, when the walk-in wardrobe, or dressing room, once again became a necessity for the storage of apparel.

OST of the bedrooms at Blenheim are enfilade and run around the east and south façades. They were originally designed and built without bathrooms but with a dressing room or antechamber, which would have been used as a private sitting room. That layout is not practical today and would be deemed a waste of space in most houses. At Blenheim, the tradition of having a separate suite of a main guest bedroom with adjacent dressing room or smaller bedroom continues, as there is no other practical use for these smaller rooms, as it is impossible to add plumbing to create en-suite bathrooms.

Some of the bedrooms are built around internal courtyards, such as the one shown here. This particular suite, adjacent to the nursery, was originally used by my dear nanny and her husband. It is now used as a guest bedroom with dressing room or child's bedroom next door. Ironically the smaller room has the better view over the North Courtyard whilst the larger bedroom looks over an internal courtyard so it is quite dark. It was decorated in warm, glowing colours to add warmth. The four-poster bed had not been used in years and was relegated to a storeroom. The bed was restored specifically for this room and has changed the ambience completely from a dull secondary space to a romantic guest suite.

above *View from the guest bedroom, which was originally used by my nanny, towards the newly formed en-suite bathroom. The room looks over an internal courtyard and not much light floods in, so warm colours were used to make it feel cosier.*

above right *A single bedroom next door was originally my sister's bedroom. It is now the dressing room, and has lovely arched windows overlooking the North Courtyard.*

opposite *The four-poster bed makes a statement. The game bird chintz gives a country feel and is used on both bed and main curtains.*

TODAY we probably spend less waking time in our bedroom than in any other room in the house, so its prime objective is to be peaceful and calming to ensure a good night's sleep.

Obviously the bed will be the focal point and take up the most space, so its position is vital. In reality there is often only one wall on which the bed can sit but if you have a choice, consider the view from the bed and the ease of reaching the door to the bathroom. My preference is not to have built-in wardrobes in the bedroom, as antiques or free standing furniture add more character.

The bedroom is a personal space so the choice of colour and fabric should reflect what makes you calm and happy.

Typically and historically the bedroom is a feminine space but a minimalist look is often more appropriate for a couple. I like to have a blue bedroom as I find it calming and restful, and although blue can be considered cold, it warms up when the right shade is used with complementary colours.

There are many styles of beds and many ways to treat them, whether a four poster, wooden frame such as a *lit bateau* or a divan with painted head- and footboard, or a brass frame. Space and ceiling height will somewhat dictate your choice, then the look and budget. Four posters are elegant yet cosy, typically a show of status and wealth, but can be claustrophobic and overpowering in a small room. As antique beds were much smaller than beds today, I often just use the posts and maybe the headboard and have the frame and cornice made. Plain beds can be treated with a half tester or corona with fabric draperies fixed to the wall to dress the bed. Whatever you choose, invest in a good-quality mattress and make the bed comfortable.

left *This attic-style bedroom with old oak beams and rafters is actually in a new wing of an older house.*

opposite top *In this smart bedroom at Babington House Hotel, the free-standing bath is luxuriously positioned in front of the fireplace.*

opposite bottom *The bedroom of an Earthship house, where emphasis is placed on using recycled materials.*

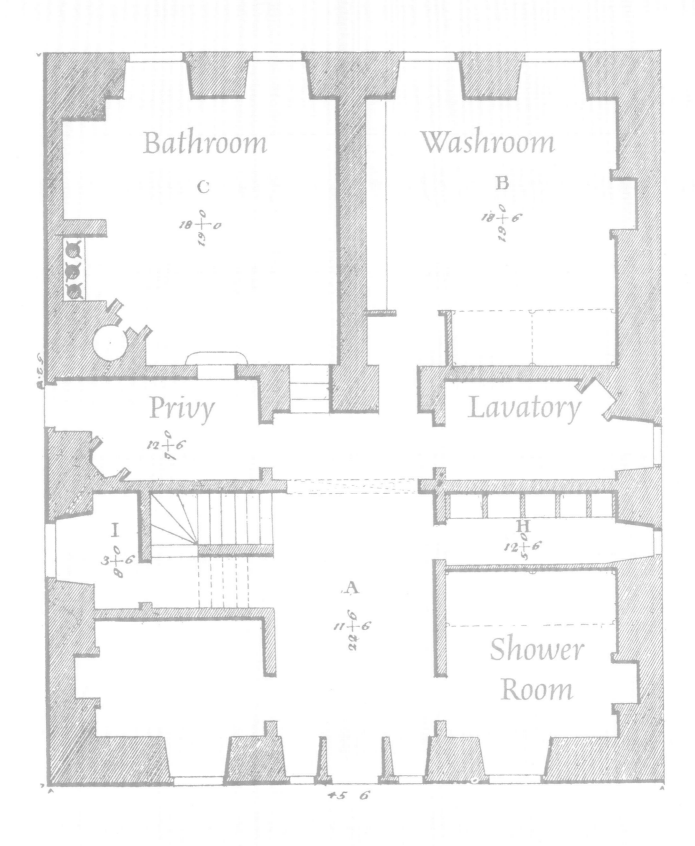

Bathroom
C
$18+0$
$19+0$

Washroom
B
$18+6$
$19+0$

Privy
$12+0$
$9+6$

Lavatory

I
$3+0$
$8+6$

H
$12+0$
$5+6$

A
$11+6$
$22+6$

Shower
Room

45 6

BATHROOMS

previous page, left and below *Free standing bathing facilities before the days of plumbing: a wonderful shower at Erddig Hall, near Wrexham in Wrexham. A hip bath in the bedroom at Carlyle's house in London – but water was delivered by housemaids from the basement kitchen. An elegant Spode bidet in a wooden table frame in the dressing room at Berrington Hall, Herefordshire.*

above *A built-in wooden seat that cleverly disguises the wc pan. This seat was used by Sir Winston Churchill on his frequent visits to Ditchley Park and has a beautiful view over the park.*

THE bathroom is a recent luxury. Until the sixteenth century, only royal palaces or monasteries had any form of running water, channeled to the house from a local spring or stream via ducts of stone or wood. The privy-shaft was the earliest form of lavatory – an opening over a shaft in the outer wall that could be flushed with a jug of rain water into a channel below ground. The close-stool was simply a wooden seat over a pot that would be emptied by staff.

By the late seventeenth century, grand houses had the option of a bathing or *bagnio* room, typically placed on the ground floor below the main bedroom and relying on gravity to feed water pumped from a nearby cistern. The one at Blenheim was one of the earliest examples, built in the 1720s for the first Duchess with hot and cold running water.

Bathrooms were expensive, so most people relied on staff to deliver hot and cold water to their bedroom or dressing room. Outdoor closets were preferable to indoor ones, as they were easier to maintain and less of a health risk. As people became more health conscious, the fashion for cold baths evolved, taken in an internal plunge pool or an ornamental grotto or bath house in the garden.

Improvements and advancements in sanitation occurred in the late eighteenth century with the invention by Joseph Bramah in 1777 of a water closet with a lever-operated flap to dispose of waste. Water was now pumped into the house mechanically and stored in tanks in the roof, allowing for gravity to feed water to baths and water closets. The bathroom as such was in an adjacent room and next to the dressing room with a deep hip bath like a slipper bath or a shower bath which elaborately dispersed hot and cold water.

left The State Dressing Room at Kingston Lacy has a wonderfully masculine feel. When the house was built in 1663, this room would have had little more than a washstand.

below A late 19th-Century bath at Blickling Hall encased in a panelled frame. The mahogany wc is from the 1860s, and in the foreground is an unusual "sit down" weighing scales.

above *The bathroom at Dunster Castle with the masculine mahogany-panelled bath and a step to get in and out easily. The stone hot-water bottle was used to warm beds.*

TOWARDS the end of the nineteenth century and early 1900s, most houses were altered to accommodate bathrooms with piped running water, but the question was where to house them? Water closets/lavatories tended to stay as separate rooms if they already existed and the male dressing room or dressing closet, which had lost its importance as separate room, was used as a bathroom. In newly built Victorian houses, it was common to have at least one bathroom on each floor – typically located on an outside wall to allow for drainage and a window for natural ventilation.

Unplanned, transitional bathrooms tended to have more character than new ones, as the bath was literally plonked in the middle of an existing room, if freestanding or, if serviced with piped water, against a wall with large crude lead pipes running haphazardly to the taps. Water had to be heated, and this was either achieved by pumping water via the kitchen range or later by the gas geyser (invented in 1868), an independent heat source that could pump hot water directly into the basin or tub. Original washstands were often wooden with a marble top and freestanding basin or bowl and matching jug placed on top. As piped water arrived, these were often altered to take taps and the basin sunk into the top.

Floors were generally wooden floorboards so rugs were added for warmth and rooms were warmed with fires and lit by gas light or candles on stands. New pieces of bathroom furniture were created, such as mahogany washstands incorporating mirrors, toilet mirrors with little drawers for storing toiletries, shaving cabinets complete with bowls and brushes and freestanding towel rails. Some older commode chairs, originally used with chamber pots, were re-vamped and placed over a flushing lavatory.

NEWLY built Victorian bathrooms were all about sanitation and hygiene, so walls and floors were tiled, if not to full height then to three-quarters, and painted in an oil-based paint above. Steam was a big problem, as the hot water could be very hot with no mixer taps to regulate the temperature and no mechanical ventilation to clear the air.

Basins were now free standing and either supported on a plain or flute pedestal, porcelain legs or a decorative metal frame. Baths too were freestanding on cast-iron legs, and all surfaces kept spartan to allow for easy cleaning. It was considered a health hazard to have curtains at the windows, or indeed fabric of any kind, so many windows had their plain glass replaced with obscure or reeded glass – another institutional touch. Although some domestic bathrooms had baths encased in wood panels and basins incorporated into wooden cabinets, the trend was still the hosed-down look with tiles on the walls and linoleum or tiles on the floor. The lavatory had undergone a huge change with the invention of the S bend, trapping a seal of water between sewer gases in the drains and the bathroom. The very latest Victorian lavatories had overhead cisterns filled with water regulated by a valve system so that water could be to be released at the pull of a chain to flush waste thought the S bend – pretty much as used today. The lavatory was still generally placed in a separate room with a wash basin. Unlike the hygienic white bath, the bowl was often elaborately painted with a floral design inside and out and typically a large wooden seat attached to the wall with iron brackets.

top *A wonderful Edwardian bath and shower at Castle Drogo, a country house built in the 1910s to designs by Edwin Lutyens. Also shown are 1910 state-of-the-art weighing scales.*

below right *The Ship Bathroom at Anglesey Abbey with marble washstand and semi built-in* WC *cistern. The marble floor with contrasting black marble skirting and simple whitewashed walls are typical of the Edwardian era.*

left *The basic bathroom at Clouds Hill showing the free-standing bathtub used by T. E. Lawrence (known as Lawrence of Arabia) and where he most probably relaxed and plotted his celebrated book* Seven Pillars of Wisdom.

THE East Wing of Blenheim has typically been the private quarters, and whilst in the early eighteenth century the first Duke and Duchess were fortunate enough to have their own bathing chamber, it was not until the late Victorian period that bathrooms were added for the convenience of the rest of the family and guests. Blenheim is built of thick solid stone and is a Grade I listed building, so it was never going to be easy to install plumbing and there was the additional problem of where to locate the bathrooms. The solution arrived at, although not ideal, was to install separate rooms suspended on a metal framework in an internal courtyard, allowing for the pipework to be more easily installed and concealed without dramatically altering the historic building. The disadvantage of these bathrooms is that you now have some very grand state bedrooms with a dressing room attached but no en-suite bathroom, as the bathroom is on the other side of the corridor. In other bedrooms, an internal bathroom has been created from what was probably a closet that has been adapted with pipes carefully concealed in internal walls and finding their way to the central drains down the stair wells of the service or back stairs.

right *This strange structure was purpose-built in the internal courtyard to provide two guest bathrooms. The roof lights let in natural light as there are no windows.*

opposite clockwise from top left

This bathroom was converted from a passage to make an en-suite bathroom. The now blocked-up window reveal was used to provide a recess for the vanity unit and glass shelves, providing useful storage.

An Edwardian bathroom installed in the 1920s. The bath panel is in wood and painted to match the marble washstand. The original flooring would have been terrazzo or linoleum and is now carpet. The room has no window but there is a roof light.

A restored Victorian style freestanding roll-top bath gives a country feel to this new en-suite bathroom. The panelling is original and picked out in blue to match the wallpaper.

THE purpose of a bathroom is to be functional, practical, warm and inviting. Wood, tile or stone floors work well in traditional bathrooms and can be used with under-floor heating. Carpets, although cosy, are not advisable; they will absorb moisture and harbor germs. Select heated towel rails to match the style of the space, from long, tall and angular to traditional and incorporating a radiator.

For a traditional look, if space permits, opt for a freestanding cast-iron roll-top bath and floor-mounted taps – if the bath needs to be located against a wall it can be boxed in with panelling. Vanity units provide valuable storage but freestanding pedestal basins look more authentic.

Showers are essential but they can ruin the look of a traditional bathroom. A separate shower room is one option, an old fashioned freestanding cubicle is another. Personally I am not a great fan of showers within the bath as they can be awkward to get in and out of and shower screens are never that effective. If this is the only option, then ensure you have head height, a non-slip finish and accessible controls.

Good lighting and mirrors are essentials, and generally speaking the combination of low-voltage down lights and wall lights work best – the key is to place them so you don't get nasty shadows and unflattering glare.

previous pages left *This newly built bathroom was originally a bedroom. The shower cubicle is new but is a copy of a Victorian one and the screen is strategically placed to hide the wc. Wood floors provide warmth and are practical if well sealed.*

right *A dressing room newly converted into a bathroom. The marble bath was hand-carved in China. The fireplace is original, and the walls hand-painted in a specialist paint finish.*

opposite, clockwise from top left

A newly renovated guest bathroom using the original restored bath and towel rail. The original terrazzo floor was cold and uninviting – the new wood plank with under-floor heating is more appealing.

A contemporary bathroom in a converted barn – the custom-made bath is filled from water coming out of the beam. The large basin is big enough for two people to use and down lights are concealed in the new beams over the mirror.

The en-suite bathroom to the bedroom seen on page 178 has specially carved bath panels and unique wood frames made for the alcoves and mirrors. The French-style pedestal basin is hand-painted.

An en-suite bathroom on the ground floor of a Tudor wing of a country house. The bath is a freestanding slipper style with floor-mounted taps, and to the right of the vanity unit is a concealed shower. The room has no window, so lighting and ventilation are important.

"I have been photographing our toilet, that glossy enameled receptacle of extraordinary beauty. Here was every sensuous curve of the 'human figure divine' but minus the imperfections."

Edward Weston (1886–1958)
American photographer

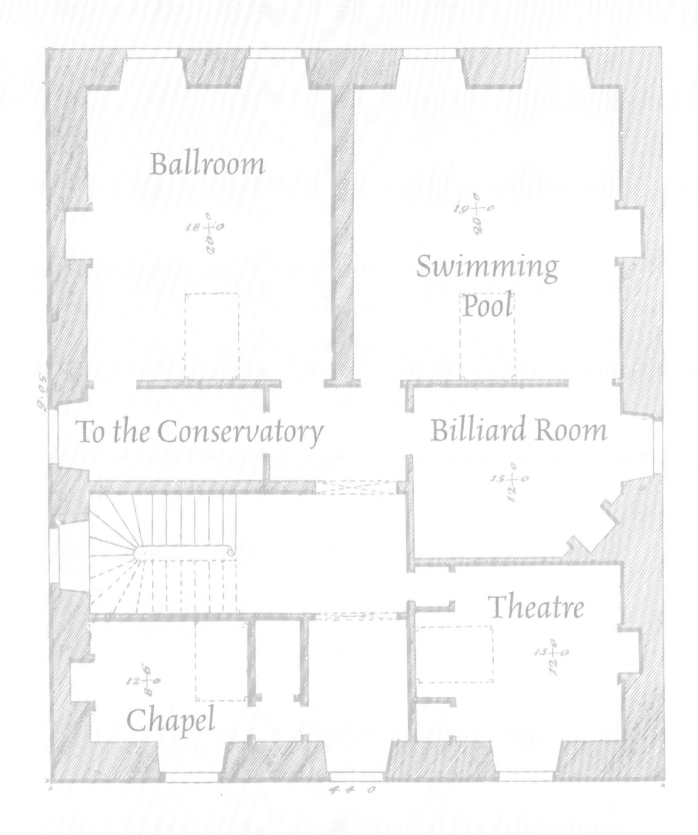

Ballroom

18 0
20 0

Swimming
Pool

19 0
20 0

To the Conservatory

Billiard Room

15 0
12 0

Theatre

15 0
12 0

Chapel

12 6
0 0

50 9

44 0

INDULGENT
ROOMS

MANY early "indulgent rooms" evolved in the eighteenth century as a result of the new middle classes wanting to show off their wealth and young men from aristocratic families returning from the Grand Tour in Europe needing somewhere to display their treasures.

Libraries were built to house books and evolved into family sitting rooms, but galleries were designed specifically to display paintings and sculpture and had little other use. Some long galleries had already been built in earlier Elizabethan and Jacobean houses for the purpose of entertaining important guests or taking exercise, but were later turned into art galleries. Today, galleries are little more than a decorative corridor, often not wide enough for any other use. Many combine books and works of art, becoming a library and gallery, like the one at Blenheim.

During the eighteenth century, when social life and entertaining reached its height, a series of substantial entertaining rooms to cater for house parties and balls was considered essential. Although it was unusual to have a designated ballroom – typically the saloon would double as a dining area to take supper and later be cleared for dancing, or the long gallery, which often ran the entire length of the house, would be used. In the nineteenth century, the numbers involved in entertaining at home grew thanks to better transportation, and larger rooms were built leading to a revival of the Great Hall, a multifunctional room for hosting family gatherings, coming-out parties, local friends and tenants and even the annual servants' party. Many of these halls had a billiard table or piano or organ and were also used to play games and perform amateur plays.

A games room was an important feature during the Victorian era when large houses had a separate billiard room to which the men – who had by now relinquished the library to the family – could retire after dinner to smoke cigars and show off their skills. Media rooms, however, seem to have superseded games rooms and large high-definition or 3-D screens with surround sound are today's number one choice of indulgent room. Indoor pools are a close second.

previous page *A view from the Sculpture Gallery at Chatsworth House which was created to house the remarkable collection of Italian sculpture collected by the 6th Duke of Devonshire in the 1820s. This elite space was created for 'the pursuit of pleasure' – the best of reasons for an indulgent room.*

left *The Elizabethan Long Gallery at Powis Castle in Wales, decorated with the family's coats of arms by Sir Edward Herbert. Originally the room would have been used for balls as well as a gallery and in the winter for indoor exercise. It is now a sculpture gallery.*

above *The Shell Gallery at A la Ronde which looks down into the Octagon Hall. The room was decorated by the two eccentric Parminter cousins with a zigzag frieze above a clerestory of eight diamond-framed windows with reveals also lined with shells.*

opposite *The Upper Gallery at Easton Neston, built by Nicholas Hawksmoor, spans east to west and provides the perfect space to display family portraits. Originally the room may have been used for dancing but now is just an elegant gallery running between two sides of the house.*

left *The Billiard Room at Biltmore is large enough to house two tables and, although built in 1895, has the feel of a Jacobean room with the strapwork ceiling and wood-panelled walls.*

above *The Billiard Room at Tyntesfield doubles up as a hunting trophy room. It was built in the Victorian period with half-height wood panelling and has a magnificent hammerbeam roof and Gothic-style details in the windows.*

The Billiard Room at Hearst Castle, decorated in 1934 with a billiard and pool table. With tiled panel walls, a 15th-Century Spanish painted ceiling depicting scenes of courtly life and the Flemish hunting scene tapestry, the décor is an eclectic mix. The architect Julia Morgan was given the task of incorporating seamlessly into the castle a host of European architectural and artistic treasures that arrived in California in packing cases.

The Gun Room at Springhill, a 17th-Century plantation house built in Northern Ireland. The room still has the original 18th-Century wallpaper and houses some rare guns, including a long gun dating from 1680.

above *The private chapel at Burghley House, which dates back to the 16th Century, has an altar designed by Paolo Veronese and carvings by Grinling Gibbons. The family would have prayed there on a regular basis whilst household staff were confined to the antechapel.*

opposite *The private chapel at Blenheim was commissioned by Sarah, 1st Duchess of Marlborough, after the death of her husband John in the 1720s. The tomb was designed by William Kent and carried out by Michael Rysbrack for £2,200 and is a memorial to the first Duke and Duchess and their two sons who died. The pews are from the Victorian era.*

*The private movie theatre built at
Hearst Castle for the newspaper magnate
William Randolph Hearst between 1919 and
1947 by the architect Julia Morgan. The style
is a pastiche of many European grand styles
and the theatre has a Baroque look. Hearst
would watch movies there every night with
his house guests, in particular the film star
Marion Davies.*

"My buildings will be my
legacy ... they will speak for
me long after I'm gone."

Julia Morgan (1872–1957)
American architect and creator of
Hearst Castle

below *The Bath Assembly Rooms, designed by John Wood the Younger in 1769, was the hub of fashionable Georgian society in the city where locals and visitors would gather for balls, social gatherings and public functions.*

opposite *The private theatre at Chatsworth was converted from the ballroom or banqueting room in the East Wing by the 8th Duke with the help of William Hemsley in 1896. It could seat two hundred guests and Edward VII was a frequent visitor, thus the theatre was referred to as the "Theatre Royal".*

"To sit in the shade on a fine day, and look upon verdure is the most perfect refreshment."

Jane Austen (1775–1817)
English novelist

above left *The exterior view of the Orangery at Blenheim which was originally used to house the orange and lemon trees in the winter. In 1787 the 4th Duke of Marlborough used the room as a private theatre and, following a fire in 1861, the new Victorian iron rib and girder roof was installed, as seen today.*

left *The interior of the Orangery, which is no longer used to house plants but as very popular venue for wedding receptions, conferences, fairs etc. The light-filled venue overlooks the Italian gardens.*

opposite *The Winter Garden at Biltmore House is attached to the house yet sunken into the ground with a spectacular Gothic-style timber roof and stone arches leading from the house and to the garden. The centre stone fountain supports a bronze by the Viennese artist Karl Bitter. The room is multifunctional and has been used for family gatherings.*

The indoor pool at Hearst Castle, called the Roman Pool, is modeled on ancient Roman baths and lined with mosaic tiles in a blue-and-gold colour scheme inspired by the Mausoleum of Galla Placidia in Ravenna. The statues are of Roman gods, goddesses and heroes.

The Folly at Wimpole Estate in Cambridgeshire designed by Sanderson Miller in 1751 is a good example of early Gothicism and looks older than it is. Perhaps the ultimate indulgence, a folly is defined in the Oxford English Dictionary *as "a costly ornamental building with no practical purpose, especially a tower or mock-Gothic ruin built in a large garden or park".*

— *ACKNOWLEDGEMENTS* —

The author and publishers would like to thank all those who have kindly allowed their houses to be photographed and featured in this book and many other locations and organisations for their cooperation and use of images.

The author would like to express her thanks to the following:

Claire White – my assistant whose meticulous work on the photography research and organization has been invaluable and carried out with great patience and flair.

Robert Dalrymple – for the beautiful layout and design that makes the book come alive.

Christopher Drake – the photographer of the specially commissioned photographs.

Conrad Villamar – for drawing the endpapers.

Alexandra Parsons – my wonderful editor, whose wit and enthusiasm never ceases – which is fortunate as this is our eleventh book together.

For Rizzoli – Ellen Nidy and Charles Miers, who have been as enthusiastic as we have been about this new project.

Front Jacket Christopher Drake

Page 2 Christopher Drake
Page 6 Roelof Bakker
Page 9 Christopher Drake
Pages 10–11 Christopher Drake
Page 12 © NTPL / Rupert Truman
Page 13 Christopher Drake
Pages 14–15 Photograph by
Jarrold Publishing. Reproduced
with the kind permission of His
Grace the Duke of Marlborough,
Blenheim Palace Image Library
Page 16 Richard Holttum
Page 17 Photograph by Jarrold
Publishing. Reproduced with the
kind permission of His Grace the
Duke of Marlborough, Blenheim
Palace Image Library
Pages 18–19 Christopher Drake
Page 21 Top Right: © NTPL / Stephen
Robson
Top left: © NTPL / John Blake
Bottom: Richard Holttum
Page 22 © NTPL / Michael Boys
Pages 24–25 Denbighshire
Heritage Service
Page 26 Adam Middleton /
The Ditchley Foundation
Page 27 Adam Middleton /
The Ditchley Foundation
Page 28 Left: Christopher Drake
Right: Ellen Leslie
Page 29 © NTPL / Robert Morris
Page 30 Ellen Rooney
Page 31 Ellen Rooney
Page 32 Top: Courtesy of Historic New
England
Bottom: Natalia Bratslavsky
/ Shutterstock
Page 33 Millford Plantation, 1841,
Sumter County, South Carolina Courtesy
of Richard Hampton Jenrette and
Classical American Homes Preservation
Trust Photograph by Van Jones Martin
Pages 34–35 © NTPL / Stuart Cox
Page 36 Left: Iain Parsons
Right: Frank Lloyd Wright School
of Architecture as the designer Bill
Timmerman as the photographer
Page 37 Top: Frank Lloyd Wright School
of Architecture as the designer Bill
Timmerman as the photographer
Bottom: Kirsten Jacobsen,
Earthship Biotecture

Page 39 Christopher Drake
Page 40 Christopher Drake
Page 42 Top Right: Christopher
Drake
Top Left: Christopher Drake
Bottom: Coloured visual by Alexandre
Serebrikoff / Ditchley Foundation
Page 43 Christopher Drake
Page 44 Left: Portrait by Sir Joshua
Reynolds. Reproduced with the kind
permission of His Grace the Duke of
Marlborough, Blenheim Palace Image
Library
Right: Coloured visual of the Great
Hall by Alexandre Serebrikoff
/ Ditchley Foundation
Page 45 Coloured visual of the
Great Hall by Alexandre Serebrikoff
/ Ditchley Foundation
Page 46 © NTPL / David Garner
Page 47 © corbettphotography.net
Page 49 Christopher Drake
Pages 50–51 Christopher Drake
Page 52 Left and right:
Christopher Drake
Page 53 Left and right:
Christopher Drake
Page 54 Christopher Drake
Page 55 Christopher Drake
Page 56 © corbettphotography.net
Page 57 Top: Photograph by Jarrold
Publishing. Reproduced with the kind
permission of His Grace the Duke of
Marlborough, Blenheim Palace Image
Library
Bottom: © NTPL / Nadia Mackenzie
Pages 58–59 © Rachael Smith
Page 60 Top Left: Christopher Drake
Top Right: No credit necessary
Bottom Left: Richard Holttum
Bottom Right: Christopher Drake
Page 61 James R. Lockhart
Pages 62–63 Christopher Drake
Page 64 Christopher Drake
Page 65 Andrew Wood
and © Cico Books
Page 66 Top: Photograph by Jarrold
Publishing. Reproduced with the kind
permission of His Grace the Duke of
Marlborough, Blenheim Palace Image
Library
Bottom Left: Photograph by Jarrold
Publishing. Reproduced with the kind
permission of His Grace the Duke of
Marlborough, Blenheim Palace Image
Library

Bottom Right: Photograph by
Jarrold Publishing. Reproduced
with the kind permission of His
Grace the Duke of Marlborough,
Blenheim Palace Image Library
Page 67 Left: Andrew Wood and © Cico
Books
Right: Richard Holttum
Page 68 © NTPL / Dennis Gilbert
Page 69 Top: © NTPL / Dennis Gilbert
Bottom: Kirsten Jacobsen,
Earthship Biotecture
Page 70 Christopher Drake
Page 71 Top: Christopher Drake
Bottom Right: Christopher Drake
Bottom Left: Christopher Drake
Page 72 Jason Oleniczak
Page 73 © NTPL / Dennis Gilbert
Page 74 Rotunda of Millford
Planation, 1841, Sumter County, South
Carolina Photographer Mr. Van
Jones Martin; courtesy of Richard
Hampton Jenrette and Classical
American Homes Preservation Trust
Page 75 James R. Lockhart
Page 76 Top Left: Jason Oleniczak
Top Right: Christopher Drake
Bottom: © Rachael Smith
Page 77 © Rachael Smith
Page 79 Christopher Drake
Page 80 Christopher Drake
Pages 82–83 Roeloff Bakker
Page 84 © NTPL / Geoffrey Frosh
Page 85 © NTPL / Geoffrey Frosh
Page 86 © NTPL / Geoffrey Frosh
Page 87 Top: © NTPL / Andreas von
Einsiedel
Bottom: © NTPL / Geoffrey Frosh
Page 88 © NTPL / Geoffrey Frosh
Page 89 © NTPL / Geoffrey Frosh
Page 90 © Country Life
Pages 92–93 © Holkham Estate
Page 94 Christopher Drake
Page 95 Top: Visual by Alexandre
Serebrikoff / Ditchley Foundation
Bottom: Christopher Drake
Page 96 Photo by James R. Lockhart
Page 97 © NTPL / Andreas von Einsiedel
Page 98 No credit necessary
Page 99 Top: No credit necessary
Bottom: Christopher Drake
Page 100 Christopher Drake
Page 101 Christopher Drake

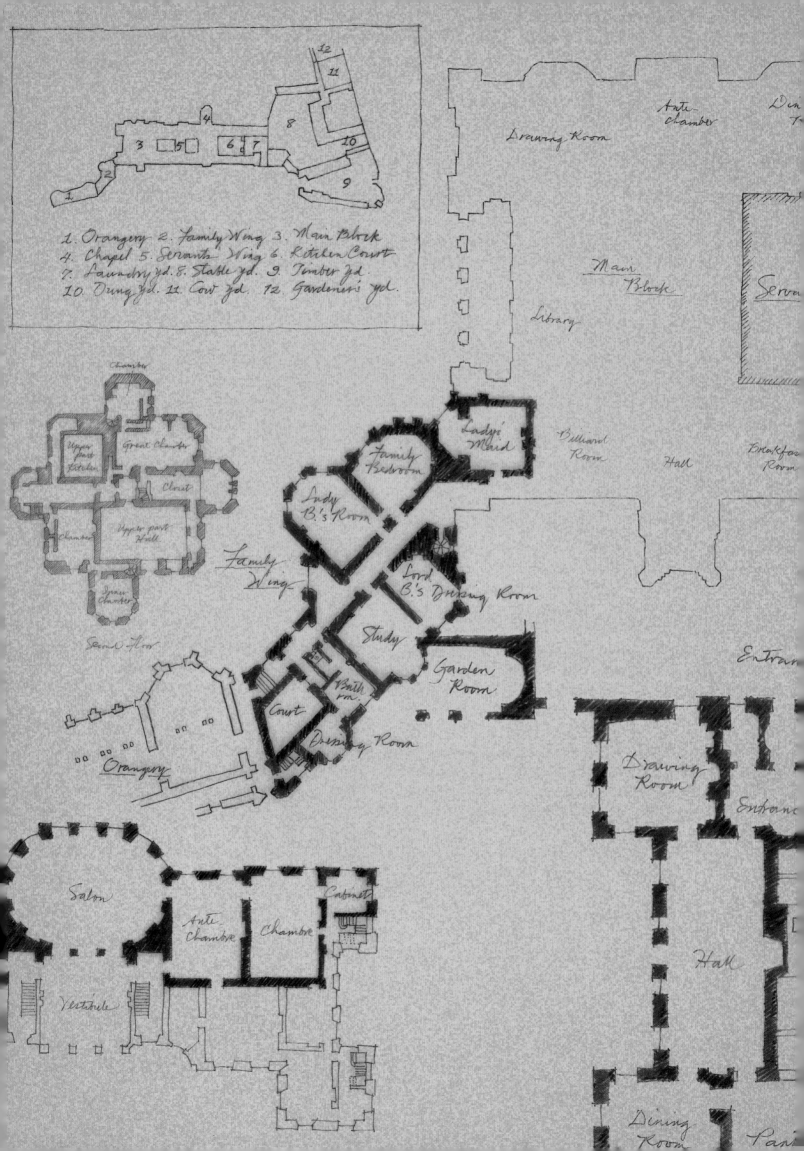

Key plan (top left):

1. Orangery 2. Family Wing 3. Main Block
4. Chapel 5. Servants' Wing 6. Kitchen Court
7. Laundry Yd. 8. Stable Yd. 9. Timber Yd.
10. Dung Yd. 11. Cow Yd. 12. Gardener's Yd.

Drawing Room

Ante-chamber

Din...

Main Block

Library

Serva...

Billiard Room

Hall

Breakfast Room

Second Floor plan (left):

Chamber

Upper part Kitchen

Great Chamber

Closet

Chamber

Upper part Hall

Inner Chamber

Second Floor

Centre plan:

Lady's Maid

Family Bedroom

Lady B.'s Room

Family Wing

Lord B.'s Dressing Room

Study

Garden Room

Bath rm.

Court

Dressing Room

Orangery

Entrance

Drawing Room

Entrance

Bottom plan:

Salon

Cabinet

Ante-Chambre

Chambre

Vestibule

Hall

Drawing Room

Dining Room

Pan...